CREATIVE CONTAINERS

The Resourceful Crafter's Guide

JILL EVANS

Published by

Krause Publications
700 E. State St.,
Iola, WI 54990-0001
www.krause.com

Please call or write for our free catalog of publications. Our toll-free number to place an order or obtain a free catalog is 800-258-0929 or please use our regular business telephone 715-445-2214.

The following photographs were taken by Photographic Solutions, Orem, Utah: Groovy wired candleholders, bridal shower wedding cake decoration, wedding reception, beverage cup birdhouses, Sammy scarecrow, witchy poo, count fangs, Perry penguin, and Rodney reindeer.
All project designs and illustrations by Jill Evans.

Library of Congress Catalog Number: 2001097826

ISBN: 0-87349-379-6

The following products and materials have been used and/or mentioned in this book:
Q-tips® brand cotton swabs; Ellison Educational Inc.® die cuts; Provo Craft® specialty scrapbook papers; Scrap In A Snap theme scrapbook kits, papers, and stickers; Doodle Bug Design Inc.™ sticker sheets by Cynthea Sandoval; Making Memories Little Letters Stickers; Paper Adventures scrapbook papers; Creative Memories® Collection die cuts; Pebbles in my Pocket custom die cuts; Mrs. Grossman's® stickers; Sandy Lion Sticker Designs®; me & my BIG ideas Sticker Designs®; Elmer's® Products, Inc. sparkle pens; Velcro® Sticky Back® Tape by Velcro USA Inc.; Royal Coat® Decoupage Finish and Apple Barrel Colors® by Plaid® Enterprises, Inc.; AM Twist® American Twisting Company; Wrights® decorative fabric trims; Delta Technical Coatings, Inc.; Delta Ceramcoat acrylic paints; STYROFOAM® is a trademark of The Dow Chemical Company, STYROFOAM® brand foam products; Fiskars® Paper Edgers and scissors; Loew-Cornell, Inc. paint brushes; Avery® Dennison Corporation office products; Springs Home Springs Bath Fashions; Coordinates Collage Decorative wall border; DecoArt, Inc.; Snow-Tex paint; Crafter's Pick™ by API; The Adhesive Products, Inc.; Aleene's® 2 in 1 Glue™ by Duncan Enterprises; Palmer® Paint Products, Inc.; Prism™ Acrylic Glow in the Dark paint; Sharpie® Markers by Stanford®; Hallmark Cards©, Inc.; Expressions gift wrap; Darice® Pearl berries floral pick; Kreative Foam™ by Design A Line Inc. molded craft foam products; Krylon® Products Group Interior/Exterior metallic spray paints and artist sprays; Dixie® bathroom cups.

ACKNOWLEDGMENTS

I would be truly ungrateful if I did not acknowledge appreciation to my family and good friends for their support and assistance. I extend my appreciation, especially, to my husband Frank for all his loving support, my friend Katherina Christiansen for her listening ear and suggestions, to my sister Lori Rager for her efforts, my brother Shelby Sanders, to Eli Escamilla and his wife Michelle for their wonderful advice and help, and to Robert Evelyn for his professional help. Also, most sincerely, my appreciation goes to the professional and exceptional staff of Krause Publications for all their efforts and contributions in publishing. And, most of all, I'd like to thank a watchful, gracious, and loving Father in Heaven who blesses me and my family in every way. Without all of this support and guidance, I would not have been able to create and complete *Creative Containers: The Resourceful Crafter's Guide.*

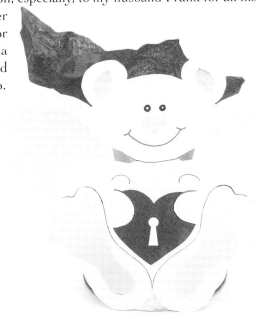

Dear Fellow Creative Craft Artist,

COME JOIN THE FUN!

Whether you're creating the projects for yourself, for family crafting fun, for school instruction, as decorations, gift containers, or even for resale at a craft boutique or bazaar—these projects are fast, easy, and fun to put together. And, hopefully, they're as affordable as crafting gets!

My main objective in designing and offering the projects in this book was to re-emphasize recycling, economy, and creativity, while offering a variety of holiday themes and home decor projects. I hope this book helps you save money by recycling and utilizing the craft materials you already have. I encourage you to use your creativity and imagination and to incorporate the items into your own original creations.

Recycling, covering a can, and using discarded items in crafting are not new concepts by any means. But, I hope to renew your interest and imagination in this area.

I, myself, am an impatient crafter. I want to make and finish my projects fast. As a mother of three small children, actively involved in my community and continuing my education, I have a small window of time to sit down and enjoy making crafts for myself or even with my children.

I thought about other crafters who might be like myself—seeking fast, fun, and creative craft projects that don't cost a fistful of money to obtain all the needed materials and supplies. I've come up with some of my own designs that I would like to share with you, as well as some suggestions to encourage you to stretch and push your imagination into creating your own projects.

My family has enjoyed creating these recycled decorative containers and filling them full of homemade cookies, popcorn, and other treats to give to neighbors, grandparents, friends, and even out into our community as gifts for others who might not otherwise be on the receiving end during holiday seasons.

Gather your crafting tools and come jump right on in for an affordable, creative, and fun time.

Your friend,

Jill D. Evans

CONTENTS

Chapter 2—Spring & Summer

Chapter 3—Halloween & Fall Harvest

Chapter 4—Winter Holiday

GETTING STARTED

Get Creative! You can incorporate just about any crafting technique or medium into your recycled cans, containers, and boxes. Some suggestions are rubber stamping, embossing, stickers, paper-punch art, die cuts, silhouette paper cuts, laser-cut motifs, stenciling, chalks, decorative painting, decoupage, foam craft shapes, embossed vellum, 3-D paper sculpture, or use your computer to print out a design. If you can create it on paper or fabric, you can put it on your container. The possibilities are truly endless.

Most of the projects shown are covered with leftover gift wrap, colored butcher paper, poster board, colored card stock, construction paper, or pieces of specialty preprinted scrapbook paper. I use my scrapbooking tools and supplies a lot! With the wide variety of die cuts, stickers, and specialty papers available, you can modify or decorate to match any theme.

Explore and Experiment with project materials and instructions. The materials and instructions are given only as a guide. It is my hope and objective that you will get excited and explore your imagination and creativity. Act upon those sudden thoughts of "Wouldn't this look cool?" or "What if I used this, instead?"

The belief that all great and professional artists produce their wonderful works of art on their first attempt is a big myth. They have explored, experimented, and practiced with all sorts of methods, colors, and materials to achieve their masterpieces. So can you!

Remember to Save your paper, plastic, and metal containers and miscellaneous packaging. Really look at and study the items that you are discarding. Could you possibly find another creative use for them? Look at the shape of the item; does it remind you of something else? Incorporate these thoughts and ideas toward your own original designs.

I salvage a lot of materials and items bound for the trash. If I think there is a potential art, craft, or practical use for it, I save it. There is a method to my resourceful madness. Once a year, I give the items that I have left over to my local public schools, youth clubs, and camps. The teachers and leaders appreciate it! If you choose to give these items to other organizations, be sure they are *clean*, not broken, and safe for handling.

Let's Get Started! Always read through the instructions first and then gather your tools and materials. This will help you think about other materials you might have around the house that you could substitute. I can't guarantee that you will find the exact papers or craft mediums I have used. But, with each project I will share with you the name and brand of the product (if possible. Some of the papers I've had around for years and can't remember where I got them) and offer other tips, suggestions, and/or substitutions to achieve similar results. Generally, I've taken care to use products and materials that you should be able find at a local craft, paper/scrapbook, fabric, or even a discount variety store near you.

LEGEND ICONS

Beginner

(In most cases, the Beginner level is applicable to youth beginners, but may still require the assistance of an adult with painting, cutting, and gluing.)

Intermediate

 The teacher project icon indicates that the project can be photocopied at 100% for students. The students can then color the pattern/design

Advanced

with crayons, markers, or even paint and glue it in place around the recycled container. Or, a tip will be noted to make the project easier for the student.

General Can and Container Descriptions

Please, use this section to find the descriptions and dimensions for the majority of the cans and containers mentioned in the projects.

The majority of the designs are based on a #10 metal can (2 lb. coffee can). A 7" tall by 6"diameter, papier-mâché, round craft box will work well too.

#10 Metal Can—7" in height by 6" in diameter by 19 1/8" in circumference. These are generally the largest metal cans offered for consumer food products, 2 lb. coffee cans, bulk and restaurant food stock cans (some of these cans have plastic lids that come with them). A few of the projects call for these cans with their lids.

#5 Metal Can—4 1/2" in height by 6" diameter by 19 1/8" in circumference. They usually hold dry soup base, hot chocolate powder mix, or snack foods.

Larger juice or soup can—7" in height by 4 1/4" in diameter by 13 1/2" inches in circumference. These can carry a variety of food products, but typically hold pineapple juice, tomato juice, or family size soup.

1 lb. pumpkin or pie filling can—4 5/8" in height by 4" diameter.

8 oz. tomato sauce can—3" in height by 2 5/8" diameter.

14–16 oz. vegetable can—4 3/8" in height by 2 7/8" diameter.

3" diameter potato chip canisters—6 oz., 3.5 oz., and 2 oz. size.

Warnings, Basic Instructions, and Crafting Tips

Warnings

If you are under the age of twelve, adult supervision is needed when using a hot glue gun, craft/utility knifes, or sharp scissors. PLEASE, ALWAYS USE CAUTION and safety measures when using any tools, products, or materials. Always read and follow instructions exactly on paint, glue, and craft products. Good, strong, tacky craft glue could be used in place of the hot glue, but it takes a little more time to hold pieces in place.

When saving metal, tin cans, and containers that have been opened by a can opener, be sure there are no sharp, protruding edges on the inside lip of the can. If you are opening a can and you are planning to save it, after you have gone around the can once to cut open the lid, go around a second time. This helps to pinch the cut edge closely up against the inside and hopefully avoid any sharp edges. If you do have a can with sharp edges, you could try using pliers to pinch and crimp down those sharp edges. If you are unable to smooth out these edges, discard the can and save another that is safer to use for the projects.

Be sure to thoroughly wash and remove labels from containers that have held food. If the container had a meat product in it, boiling the container in water for five minutes is the best way to thoroughly clean it. I have found that many times after I have soaked labels off my containers, I can't always remove the adhesive underneath or the ink that is printed directly on the plastic containers I have used.

A good chemical or citrus adhesive remover works well on those tough spots. Again, always read the instructions when using any of these types of products. In most cases, for the projects in this book, containers will be covered completely with paper or paint.

Basic Instructions and Crafting Tips

Gluing—I've found that when working with heavier papers, like card stock or poster board, or with any project step that requires instant grab and hold, hot glue guns work best.

Paper glue sticks worked best with lighter weight papers and for a smooth look when papers are applied to each other, but they didn't work as well on the textured papers like glitter, suede, velveteen, handmade, and mulberry papers. For these surfaces, I used a strong, thick craft glue.

Painting—Spray painting should always be done outside or in a well-ventilated area. Cover your work area with newspaper, and use a large cardboard box as a shield.

Whether you use spray paint or acrylic paint, start out with a thin, even first coat, allowing enough drying time between each application. Repeat this painting process until you have complete coverage. This may take three to four applications. Always follow the manufacturer's directions.

Brush Care—Store your paintbrushes upright, and keep them from touching each other. Always thoroughly wash and clean them out quickly after each use. With good care, your brushes will last a long time.

lighthouse trio

Red Lighthouse

INTERMEDIATE

HERE IS A SIMPLE AND CHARMING LIGHTHOUSE DECORATION YOU CAN MAKE WITH A MINIMAL AMOUNT OF EFFORT. THE FINISHED DECORATION IS APPEALING BY ITSELF, OR YOU COULD MOUNT IT ON TOP OF A LARGE, FLAT ROCK WITH A LITTLE BIT OF HOBBY LICHEN OR SPANISH CRAFT MOSS.

Materials:

- 1 clean, 32 oz. paper beverage cup (7" tall x 4" diameter at the mouth of the cup)
- 4" diameter black plastic base from 16 oz. camping propane canister
- Empty, .6 oz., plastic spice container with red lid
- Red lid from an empty 2.3 oz. plastic spice container
- 11" of 1" wide red ribbon or colored paper strips
- 12" of 1 1/2" wide red ribbon or colored paper strips
- White spray paint or acrylic paint (apply with a 1" or 2" Loew-Cornell foam paintbrush)

- 1 sheet of 8 1/2" x 11" red corrugated card stock
- 1 sheet of 8 1/2" x 11" white card stock
- Fine point permanent black and red markers
- Toothpick (paint it red, using a permanent marker)
- Hot glue and strong plastic glue
- Patterns (pages 66–67)

INSTRUCTIONS

1. If you come across a plain, white, 32 oz., paper beverage cup, you can eliminate this painting step and go to step 2. If not, refer to the painting instructions on page 8. Paint your beverage cup white, covering the entire outside of the cup.

2. Turn the small .6 oz. red plastic spice container upside down. Use the plastic glue to glue the top of the lid to the center top of the larger red plastic lid. Apply glue to the underside of the rim of the larger lid, center it, and place it inside the black plastic propane base. Set aside for glue to dry and set.

3. Cut the circular lighthouse roof pattern out of the red, corrugated card stock. Fold the circular roof piece along the dotted lines, overlapping one section, to create a cone shape. Glue it in place.

4. Go back to your spice container/lids and black plastic base. Place glue around the bottom of the clear plastic container and in a little glob in the very center. Place your roof on top, centering it on the inverted clear plastic container. Cut 1/2" off the bottom of your colored toothpick, and insert it through the center point of the conical roof.

5. Light Keeper's House

a. Trace or photocopy the Light Keeper's House pattern onto white cardstock.

b. Color or paint the shaded windows and doors.

c. Cut along the solid lines. Fold in along all dotted lines.

d. Form the house into a box. Glue tab A to the inside of the house wall.

e. For the base of the house, fold the flaps like you would to close up a box. Spot glue the underside of the flaps to hold them in place.

f. Glue tabs C and D to the underside of the roof side #1.

g. Glue tabs B, E, and F to the underside of the roof side #2.

h. For the roof, cut a rectangle, 4 1/2" x 2 3/4", out of the red, corrugated card stock, preferably with the corrugated lines running horizontal with the 2 3/4" width. Fold the red card stock in half. Spread glue along the roof sides of the house. Center and glue the roof piece on top of the house.

6. Wrap your smaller strip of red ribbon around the paper cup towards the true bottom of the cup, and glue it in place where the strip overlaps or meets in the back. Repeat this same step with the wider and longer strip towards the true top of the cup.

7. Trace or photocopy two windows and a door onto white card stock. You can use the pattern choices, or try the light keeper's house patterns. Color in the windows and door shapes with a black marker, cut them out, and glue them onto your cup.

8. Glue the black plastic base to the bottom of the cup. Glue one side of the light keeper's house to the base side of your completed lighthouse.

Black Lighthouse

TEACHER Project

BEGINNER

This lighthouse is an example of another fun way to create a different look, changing just a few elements of the design. The beverage cup (main structure) remains the same as the Red Lighthouse, but the Black Lighthouse uses different colored paper, a clear plastic cup, and a handrail pattern.

MATERIALS:

- Clean, 32 oz., beverage cup (needs to have a 2 3/4" diameter at the bottom for the clear cup to fit well)
- 10 oz., clear, plastic cup 4" tall x 3" diameter (top opening)
- Cardboard toilet-paper tube, cut once vertically
- Enough aluminum foil to wrap around, cover, and tuck into the tube
- 2, 18" long strips of 3/4" black butcher paper or ribbon
- White spray paint or acrylic paint (apply with a 1" or 2" Loew-Cornell foam paintbrush)
- 8 1/2" x 12" sheet of black poster board or card stock for railing, hand rail strip, and roof
- Craft glue
- Fine point black permanent marker
- Toothpick (paint black with a permanent marker)
- Patterns (pages 66–67)

INSTRUCTIONS

1. Follow the same instructions for step one of the Red Lighthouse project.

2. Trace the roof circle and handrail patterns onto the black poster board or card stock, and cut them out. Fold the rails upward. Center and glue the handrail strip (1/4" x 11 1/4") around the middle of the rails. Turn your plastic cup upside down. Place the railing around the cup, and glue the bottom ring of the railing to the underside of the rim of the cup.

3. Fold the circular roof piece along the dotted lines, overlapping one section, and glue it in place.

4. Place glue around the bottom rim of the plastic cup, and put a little glob of craft glue in the very center. Center and place your black, conical roof on the bottom of the plastic cup. Cut 1/2" off the bottom of your colored toothpick. Insert the toothpick through the center point of the conical roof and into the glob of glue.

5. Measure and tear the black butcher paper into two 3/4" x 18" strips. Wrap the strips around the cup towards the true bottom of the cup. Glue the strips in place where they overlap or meet in the back.

6. Using the window and door patterns, trace or photocopy the

Light Keeper's House onto white card stock. Color in the windows and door shapes with a black marker, cut them out, and glue them where you would like them on your cup.

7. Cut a slit all the way up one of the toilet paper tubes. Trim 1/2" off one end of the tube, and curl it into itself to create a smaller tube with 3/4" diameter. Wrap a piece of tin foil around a couple of times, and tuck the excess foil into the ends of the tube.

8. Glue one end of the tube to the center bottom of the white beverage cup. Place glue on the top end of the foil tube. Apply glue just inside the top rim of the clear plastic cup. Turn the cup upside down, place the cup over the tube, and firmly press it down onto the bottom of the white cup.

tips SUGGESTIONS

Instead of wrapping the toilet paper tube with tin foil, use glow-in-the-dark paper or paint. Then you would have a lighthouse that truly glows at night!

Blue Lighthouse

BEGINNER

Make this beacon-of-light gift container, fill it with salt-water taffy, and give it to the seaman/woman in your life.

MATERIALS:

- 1 clean 6 oz. potato chip canister with clear plastic lid
- 1 clear, plastic, 8 oz. water/pop bottle with plastic lid
- 1 clear, plastic lid from a 15.9 oz Betty Crocker Frosting Toppers spreadable frosting
- 1 sheet of 8 1/2" x 11" off-white card stock
- Navy blue card stock strips, cut into these dimensions:
  - 1/4" x 11" strip, 1 1/2" x 11" strip, 1 1/8" x 11" strip, 5/8" x 11" strip
  - 1" x 9" strip for the base around the light glass (water bottle), and 2 3/4" diameter circle for roof cover over bottle lid
  - 5/8" x 4 1/2" strip of navy blue corrugated paper stock
- Fine point blue and black permanent markers

- Hot glue, strong craft glue, and paper glue stick
- Toothpick cut to 1 1/4" long (paint with a permanent blue marker)
- 3 1/2" x 4 1/2" piece of silver foil card stock or silver gift paper
- 2" square piece of black construction paper
- Patterns (pages 66–67)

INSTRUCTIONS

1. Wrap the off-white paper around the potato chip canister. Push the edge of the paper right up to the rim at the top, and glue in place.

2. Wrap the 1/4" x 11" navy blue card stock strip around the exposed bottom of the canister, and glue it in place. Wrap the 1 1/2" x 11" navy blue strip near the bottom of the canister, and glue it in place. Continue with the 1 1/8" and 5/8" x 11" navy blue strips. Wrap and glue the 1" x 9" navy blue color strip around the base of the half pint water bottle.

3. Glue or color small black window shapes on the canister, anywhere you wish.

4. Using the diagram and pattern guide for reference, trace and cut the 2 3/4" roof circle out of navy blue card stock. Cut the solid lines all the way around the roof circle. Gently fold each one of the

1/4" tabs toward the center. Start overlapping the pie-shaped area edges to form a slight cone. Glue the edges of the roof circle to hold the cone form.

5. Place a glob of craft glue on top of the plastic lid of the water bottle. This will anchor the toothpick.

6. The tabs will overhang and need to be glued to the outside area of the plastic lid. Wrap and glue the 5/8" x 4 1/2" strip of navy blue corrugated paper around the tabs and outside edge of the lid. Poke a hole at the center dot of the cone roof, and insert the toothpick through the hole.

7. Curl the 3 1/2" x 4 1/2" silver foil card stock to form a tube, and glue the edges in place. Slide the tube into the bottle, and screw the lid back on.

8. Center the bottom of the plastic water bottle inside the inverted frosting lid, and glue it down. Glue the bottom of the frosting lid to the top of the potato chip canister's plastic lid. Set aside for glue to dry and set.

9. Fill with candies.

Kokopeli can

Here is a decorative container to hold a plant or present a gift of goodies to a Southwestern collector friend.

Special Tools Needed:

- Wire cutters
- 1/8" hole punch

Materials:

- 1 clean #10 can
- 2 sheets of scrapbook paper, cut to 6 3/4" x 11" or a single piece of 6 3/4" x 20" gift wrap
- Double-sided gold/silver poster board
- 64" silver-colored #20 gauge wire
- Knife
- Hot glue or tacky craft glue
- Kokopeli pattern (page 64)

Instructions

1. Wrap the paper around the can, and glue it in place where the paper overlaps itself.

2. Trace three right-facing Kokopeli patterns on the gold side of the poster board. Trace three left-facing patterns on the silver side. Cut out the designs. Use a craft/utility knife to cut out the inner shapes, near the head and between the arms.

3. Use the 1/8" hole punch to punch out the eyeholes

4. Place glue on the center back of the head, center of the back, and center of the skirt of the Kokopeli designs. Press the designs onto the can, alternating silver and gold. I placed the silver ones up higher and the gold ones down lower, so the edges stick out and away from the curved surface of the can. (If you chose to use craft glue, you will need to let it dry and set before you continue to step 5.)

5. With the wire cutters, cut 64" of wire. Randomly wrap and bend the wire around the can, weaving and catching the wire in and out of the raised edges of the Kokopeli designs. I found 64" went around twice, and then I just hooked about 1/2" from the beginning of the wire around the last 1/2" of the end.

tips & SUGGESTIONS

You could use metallic foil card stock (available in scrapbook supply stores), light-weight chipboard, or cardboard in place of the double-sided silver/gold poster board. (I save chipboard/cardboard from pantyhose, clothing packaging, cereal boxes, the backing off paper writing tablets, etc.)

If you decide to use the lightweight chipboard, you then need to paint three right-facing Kokopeli (gold) and three left-facing Kokopeli (silver).

Moose can

MATERIALS:

- 1 clean #10 can with lid
- 2 sheets of 8 1/2" x 11" sage-colored card stock
- Moose die cut in brown card stock (I used Ellison die cuts)
- Primitive fir tree die cuts in forest green card stock paper (I used Ellison die cuts)
- Beige- or tan-colored chalk or chalk pastel
- Brown permanent marker

INSTRUCTIONS

1. Measure, cut, and glue the sage-colored card stock to create a 6 3/4" x 20" background paper.

2. Using a brown marker, mark a crisscross border along the top and bottom of the sage-colored background paper.

3. Glue the background paper around the can.

4. Lightly chalk the edges of the moose's legs, muzzle, antlers, and goatee. Rub the chalk with your finger to smooth it out.

5. Glue your die cut pieces in place on the front of your can.

6. Tuck some decorative tissue paper into the can, and fill it with a gift.

This is an easy gift container made with leftover die cuts from scrapbooking. Fill it with tasty treats for that outdoors man/woman or hunter in your life.

tips & SUGGESTIONS

This project could be done with whatever scrapbook paper supplies and die cuts you have. Any theme goes—how about repeating a favorite scrapbook page design to be recreated on a can and given as a gift? Using die cut paper dolls in a decorated career motif would be another idea. Create a police officer theme, cover the can, and fill it with doughnuts for your favorite police officer, as a gift of gratitude for their service. What about a fireman, a nurse, doctor, teacher, or clergyman?

Pressed leaves desk set

MATERIALS:

- 1 clean vegetable can
- 1 family-sized soup or tomato juice can
- Natural-colored, handmade paper cut to:
  - 6 1/2" x 11 1/2" for the vegetable can size
  - 8 1/2" x 14" for the family size soup can
- Decoupage medium (I used Royal Coat Decoupage Finish by Plaid)
- Collect small, pressed autumn leaves in different colors, or all green leaves in a variety of shapes and sizes (Artificial silk leaves can be used as well, just peel the plastic stemming off the backsides.)

INSTRUCTIONS

1. Wrap the paper around the cans, and glue it in place where the paper overlaps itself. Fold and wrap the overlapping 1/2" edges over the top and bottom, and glue the edges to the inside and bottom of the cans.

2. Arrange the leaves how you would like them to appear on the cans. Random directions and overlapping help give a more natural look.

3. Working one leaf at a time, use your brush to apply the decoupage medium in a thin, but complete, coat on the back side of the leaf. Press and apply the leaf to the can. Repeat this step with each leaf, until you cover the cans.

4. Once the leaves are all in place, brush a thin coat of decoupage medium over the top

THESE bRiNG THE look of NATURE iNTO A ROOM. WHAT AbOUT fiNdiNG SOME bRASS cANdlE dRip shiElds THAT ARE A liTTlE lARGER THAN THE cANs' diAMETERs? PlAcE THEM ON TOp of yOUR fiNishEd dEcOupAGE cANs, ANd NOW yOU hAVE SOME iNTRiGuiNG cANdlEhOldERs.

of the leaves and paper. Allow the cans to dry.

5. Once dry and clear, brush a second thin coat of decoupage medium over the cans. Allow it to dry thoroughly.

tips   SUGGESTIONS

You could use pressed, dried flowers, silk flowers (with the plastic stem support removed), old stamps, pictures of leaves, flowers cut from magazines, designs from fabric, or whatever your heart desires. You could try making your own decoupage medium by thinning white school glue with water until it is thin enough to paint with—make sure it's the kind that dries clear. Experiment with this homemade version until you are satisfied with the results. Be sure to allow each coat to dry thoroughly before applying the next coat.

bathroom essentials holders

THESE HANDY CONTAINERS ARE SUPER EASY TO MAKE, AND YOU CAN MODIFY OR DECORATE THEM TO MATCH ANY BATHROOM THEME. USE THEM TO HOLD COTTON BALLS, Q-TIPS, HAIR ELASTICS, TOOTHBRUSHES, ETC. THEY ALSO MAKE GREAT PENCIL/PEN HOLDERS.

MATERIALS:

- 1 clean, 12 oz., white frosting container with white lid
- Craft/utility knife
- Hot glue or craft glue—one that holds well to plastic
- 20 sea green decorative glass gems or pebbles
- 31 blue decorative glass gems or pebbles
- Natural seashells
- 5–7 small-to-medium shells
- 1 small starfish
- 12" border fish stickers (I used Sandy Lion Sticker Designs)
- Toothbrush holder design (page 64)

INSTRUCTIONS

1. Soak and remove the paper label from the container.

2. Natural Seashell Container—Arrange the seashells/starfish as you want them to look. Apply hot glue or plastic glue to the backsides of the shells, along the flat edges, so they will make good contact with the surface of the container. Stick them on the container. You could glue one or a few on top of the lid.

3. Fish Stickers Container—You can use any choice of stickers. Take a border strip of stickers, and slowly apply it to the container by wrapping it around so the stickers don't wrinkle.

4. Toothbrush Holder—

a. Remove the lid and mark four to six 1" circles around the center and 1 1/2" in from the outer edge of the lid. Use the diagram as a guide. If the holder is for children's toothbrushes, some of the new sculptured character brushes have very wide handles. You might want only four 1 1/2" circle holes for these.

b. Place scrap cardboard underneath the lid to protect the underlying surface. Very carefully, use a craft knife to cut out the holes (*kids, get help from an adult*). Place the lid back on the container.

c. Using your hot glue or plastic glue, apply glue to the backside and flat edge of the glass pebbles/gems. Apply them in whichever way you like. Leave room at the top, so you will be able to remove the lid to clean out the container.

tips SUGGESTIONS

You can decorate these containers with just about anything. Use leftover wallpaper border to coordinate with the wallpaper in your bathroom. Use printed, decorative paper or kids' artwork cut to fit around your containers. *Laminate the paper strips before you apply them, so they are protected from moisture.*

faux leather bear box

If you or someone you know is into the look of mountain lodge decor, this box becomes a nice one to display or use as a gift container. From across the room, it looks like its created from hand-sewn leather with tin accents. But, it's only a mockery made out of paper!

Instructions

1. Punch out die cuts of the bear and primitive trees in the nutmeg/rusty brown card stock. Trace and cut the mountain and moon shapes (next page) out of nutmeg/rust brown card stock.

2. Place bear, trees, moon, and mountain shapes on top of scrap newspaper. With your earth-tone chalks, mark streak-looking lines on the shapes (just enough to give the feeling of rust spots and streaks on tin). Rub in the chalk with your finger. When you achieve the rusty look you want, spray the shapes with a thin, even coat of fixative, and set them aside until needed. Remember to follow the manufacturer's directions when using the fixative.

3. Cut off the overhanging edges of the shoebox lid, this should leave you with a flat piece of 8 1/4" x 11" cardboard. If you wish, cover the underside of the cardboard lid with an extra sheet of decorative paper.

4. Cut the sheets of handmade paper into sized pieces, 1" taller than the box's side heights. The pieces should overlap 1/2" into the interior and around the underside of the bottom of the box. Cut a piece to cover the top lid, overlapping 1/16" on each side. Cut a piece of paper the size of the bottom of the box.

5. Spray each side of the box, one at a time, with the spray adhesive, and adhere the matching piece of paper to that side. Fold the overlapping paper edges into the inside of the box, and glue them in place. Using craft glue, glue the edges of the overlapping paper to the bottom of the box. Glue the matching piece of paper to cover the bottom for a finished look. Spray the cardboard lid piece with the adhesive, and adhere the paper lid cover to the cardboard piece.

6. With the 1/8" hole punch, punch holes through the cardboard lid piece—1/2" from the edge, at 1" increments around the lid.

7. Punch two 1/8" holes in the center of the front side of the box, down 1/2" and down 3/4" from the top edge of the box.

8. Align the top, backside of the lid with the top edge of the back-side of the box. This is where these two edges will be hinged together with the leather lacing. Staggering the holes to the right about 1/2" from the holes punched on the lid, punch 1/8" holes—1/2" down from the top edge of the back side of the box, at 1" increments.

9. With a metal awl or penny nail, punch five holes going down along the corner sides about 1" apart and 1/2" in from the corner sides of the box. Stagger the holes from the other corner to create a diagonal stitch when the leather lacing is threaded through. Please,

remember to be cautious and go slowly when using an awl or sharp object.

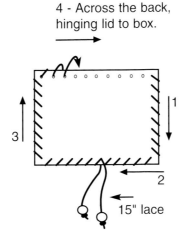

4 - Across the back, hinging lid to box.

10. Cut 4 lengths of 11" of leather lacing, 1 length of 15", and 1 length of 6". Set these aside. Using the remaining length of lacing, start threading through the underside of the first hole in the upper right hand corner of the flat lid. Tie off a knot on the underside. Wrap the lacing over the lid edge. Coming up through the next hole, continue to thread the lacing through the holes in a clockwise direction all the way around to the upper left corner of the lid. Lace leather through the first hole on the backside of the box, come up through the next hole at the back-side of the lid, continue threading

across to the right, hinging the lid to the box in this manner. Tie off and knot at the end, in the interior of the box.

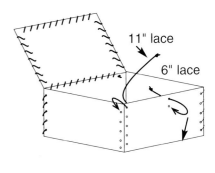

11. Take the 4 lengths of 11" lacing, and lace each of the four corners of the box in the same manner as the lid. Thread the 6" lacing through the two holes in the front side of the box, create a loop in front and tie off the ends on the inside. Thread the remaining 15" lacing through the middle hole of the top front side of the laced lid. String a bead on each end of this 15" length and tie ends to hold beads on. Push a beaded end of lacing through the loop in front of box and loosely tie together.

12. Finish by gluing the bear, moon, mountain, and tree shapes onto the top of the lid.

tiered candleholders

THIS SET OF CANDLEHOLDERS MAKES A NICE ACCENT FOR ANY ROOM. SET THEM ON A COFFEE TABLE OR SOFA TABLE. USE LEFTOVER WALLPAPER BORDER TO COORDINATE THEM WITH AN ALREADY WALLPAPERED ROOM.

MATERIALS:

- 1 clean #5 can
- 2 clean 4" diameter cans with varied heights (I used LaChoy Chinese dinner cans)
- 2, 6" diameter saucers/plates and a 7 5/8" diameter saucer /plate (I found mine at a thrift store for twenty-five cents each)
- A strong glue for metals, ceramics, etc. (I used The Ultimate Crafter's Pick by API)
- Gold spray paint or silver paint (I recommend Krylon Metallics)
- Leftover wallpaper border or preprinted scrapbook paper (I used 6 3/4" x 20" Coordinates Collage Decorative wall border by Springs Home Springs Bath Essentials)
- 1 sheet of 8 1/2" x 11" burgundy suede paper or velveteen paper
- Various candles

INSTRUCTIONS

1. Place a line of glue along the top open rims of the cans. Center the bottom of the plates on top of the can rims. Set aside, and allow the glue to dry and set.

2. Following the instructions for spray painting (page 8). Spray the cans and plates with three to four coats of gold paint.

3. Creatively cover the outer surfaces of the cans with wallpaper or printed, designed paper.

4. Place the larger home decor candles on the holders, or arrange a grouping of smaller diameter and different heights of candles together on each holder.

5. If you're using a wallpaper border that has a straight line of design patterns on the top and bottom of the border strip, trim the 1 1/4" border strip off the top and bottom of the border. Taking one of the small strips, cut it to the length of 13". Cut the other strip into four 4 3/8" lengths.

6. Use the leftover main portion of the border, 4 1/4" by 20", to wrap around the taller can, and glue in place. Take the 13" strip and wrap it around the bottom section of the shorter 4" diameter can. Glue it in place.

7. Cut and glue the burgundy/velveteen paper to make a 4 3/8" by 13" piece. Wrap and glue the paper around the 4 1/2" x 4" diameter can. Glue the remaining strips in place vertically, equally spaced around the can.

tips & SUGGESTIONS

These holders can be made with any sized cans and small plates or saucers. Be creative and try different arrangements. Check with your local wallpaper stores. Some stores will cut samples or give you small demo rolls of wallpaper and borders for you take home to see if the wallpaper will match the colors in your home. The newer, die cut edge borders in floral or fruit designs would be lovely against a solid background.

What about finding some brass candle drip shields that are a little larger than the cans' diameters? Place them on top of your finished cans.

groovy wired candleholders

THESE CANDLEHOLDERS CAN BE DECORATED TO MATCH ANY ROOM INTERIOR. USING THE MATERIALS AND INSTRUCTIONS BELOW, YOU CAN CREATE THE HOLDERS PICTURED HERE OR USE THE INSTRUCTIONS AS A GUIDE TO CREATE CANDLEHOLDERS TO SUIT YOUR OWN PERSONAL TASTE.

Special Tools Needed:

- Wire cutters
- Needle nosed pliers

Materials:

- 1 clean 6 oz. potato chip canister
- 1 clean 2 oz. potato chip canister
- Gold spray paint
- 2, 4 1/2" diameter plastic doll plates, small saucers, or brass candle shields
- 2 sheets of 8 1/2" x 11" metallic blue foil card stock cut to:
  - 10 1/2" x 8 1/2"
  - 3" x 10"
- #20 gauge copper or gold-colored wire cut into:
  - 6, 26" lengths
  - 6, 12" lengths
  - 24, 1" lengths (wire connectors)
- Contact adhesive cement or glue (I used The Ultimate Crafter's Pick by API)
- Hot glue
- Wire guide (page 65)

Instructions

1. Remove plastic lids from the potato chip canisters (save for another use). Center and glue the bottom of the plastic plates to the top opening rims of the two canisters. Set aside, and allow to set and dry.

2. When the glue has dried, follow the basic instructions for painting (page 8). Apply three to four coats of gold spray paint, until the canisters and plates have a complete and even coverage of paint. Set aside, and allow them to dry completely.

3. Using the wire guide, bend and curl the wire lengths into groovy 'S' shapes (the six 26" lengths make approximately 10" tall 'S's for the taller holder, and the six 12" lengths make 2 1/2" tall 'S's for the shorter holder). Layout a set of six matching 'S' wires next to each other, going every other direction.

4. Using the wire pliers, bend twenty-four 1" wire pieces into half cork screws, and place these at each point where the 'S' wires touch. You will use twelve wire connectors for each groovy wire layout. Beginning with one connection at a time, wrap the wire corkscrews around two touching wires at each connection point, and pinch them closed.

5. When you reach the last two connectors for a wire layout, gently roll the wire design into a tube and connect the end wire 'S's to each other at the two connecting points. Repeat this step for the shorter wire layout.

6. Wrap the larger piece of blue metallic foil card stock around the tallest canister. Glue it in place with hot glue. Wrap the smaller piece around the shorter canister, and glue it in place with hot glue.

7. Very slowly and gently, slide the wire design tubes up around the canister holders. If the wire design seems to loosen and slips around, spot glue the wire toward the back where the paper was seamed together.

8. Place your choice of candles on top and enjoy your creation. Nobody will know they are made out of cardboard potato chip cans … unless you tell them.

Coin sorter bank

My sweet, little neighbor friend Katelyn Nielsen gave me this idea when she asked for my help with a coin sorter bank she was trying to create. She wanted to create a bank that would separate her quarters, dimes, nickels, and pennies. We put our heads together and came up with this easy, practical, and functional bank container. My children liked it so well they each wanted their own, along with their own choice of "Cool" paper to decorate their banks.

MATERIALS:

- 1 clean, 6 oz. potato chip canister with plastic lid
- Your choice of decorative paper (one sheet 8 1/2" x 11"):
- I used a silver, holographic card stock from Hygloss Products Inc.
  - Tiger stripes printed scrapbook paper
    - Orchid Diamond dust card stock by Paper Adventures
    - 3 white, sparkle, tinsel chenille stems 12" x 15mm
- 1 sheet 8 1/2" x 11" chipboard (like the cardboard backing off a writing paper pad)
- 1, 1/2" square of Velcro Sticky Back Tape or a small Velcro dot or tab
- 1/4" curling ribbon (coordinating color to match your cover paper choice)
- Hot glue and thick craft glue
- Craft knife
- Ruler or measuring tape with 1/32" increment marks
- 1 piece of scrap, white card stock paper (cut a 1 1/2" diameter circle for cent number markings)
- Fine point black permanent marker
- Coin sorter patterns (page 68)

INSTRUCTIONS

1. Center, wrap, and glue your choice of decorative paper around the canister. Use a color coordinated ribbon or paper strip to cover any exposed parts of the canister.

2. For the Purple Canister— Bend, coil, and glue the white, sparkle chenille stems all around the canister.

3. Measure and cut two chipboard strips to 2 13/16" x 8 7/8". Measure and mark a centerline on both sides of the chip board strips. Measure, mark, and, cut one strip up to 4 7/8" on the 8 7/8" length. Then measure, mark, and cut the other strip up to 4".

4. Intersect the two chip board strips at the cuts to create an "X." Glue at intersections. Apply glue along the bottom edges of the cardboard "X," and push them down into the canister to glue in place. Allow to dry and set.

5. Trace and cut out the coin sorter cover (partial pie shape) from the leftover chip board. Flip the cover over, and attach one side of the 1/2" square of Velcro sticky back tape (or glue the small Velcro dot/tab) to the underside. Peel away the backing from the other side of the Velcro and attach it to the bottom of the potato chip canister. This cardboard shape is used to block off the other coin openings when removing one type of coin. Velcro helps to keep the coin sorter cover from getting lost; it attaches and stores on the underside of the bank canister until it is needed.

6. Using the coin-slot-guide pattern, trace the openings onto the plastic lid. Carefully cut the coin slot openings with a craft knife. Cut a 1 1/2" diameter circle out of the scrap of card stock paper. Glue the circle to the center of the lid. With a permanent marker, write the cent numbers next to the appropriate coin slot. Remember to align the coin slots over the correct and matching coin sections when you remove the lid and go to replace it.

Pet treats cans

Special Tools Needed:

- #4 shader paintbrush (I used Loew-Cornell Comfort 3300)
- #2 round paintbrush (I used Loew-Cornell #2 round Comfort 3000)

Materials:

- 2 clean #10 cans with plastic lids
- Several 8 1/2" x 11" sheets of brightly colored card stock, cut to 6 3/4" x 11"
- Acrylic paint colors or fine point opaque paint markers (I used Delta Creamcoat acrylic paints)
- Fine point black permanent marker
- Patterns (pages 69–70)

Here, Kitty, Kitty

- Bright green, blue, and purple card stock for background
- Acrylic paint colors used: Ocean reef blue #02074, Opaque yellow #02509, G.P. purple #02091, Hydrangea pink #02449

You Whistled?

- Brown card stock for background
- Acrylic paint colors used: White, Ocean reef blue #02074, Opaque yellow #02509, Hydrangea pink #02449, Crimson red #02076

These are very quick and decorative containers to hold kitty snacks and doggie treats. This project is designed to let you be creative and choose the colors you would like to paint the design.

INSTRUCTIONS

1. Photocopy or trace the pattern onto a 8 1/2" x 11" sheet of colored card stock.

2. Using acrylic paint colors or opaque paint markers, paint in the desired areas.

3. Cut paper to fit, wrap the paper around the can. Glue it in place.

4. Fill the can with Fido's or Kitty's favorite treats.

tips — SUGGESTIONS

The projects shown are just a suggestion. You could really personalize your treat can to your own pet or pets by using photos. Mat your pet's photo with a pre-cut paper frame, or create your own frame. Cover the can with a background paper, and glue the framed photo onto the can. You could add a saying or pet's name with letter stickers. Embellish the can with other stickers, rubber stamp designs, etc. It's as simple as that!

chapter 2

SPRING & SUMMER

INTERMEDIATE

larry leprechaun

MATERIALS:

- 1 clean 1 lb. pumpkin or pie filling can.
- 1 sheet of bright orange card stock, 2 pieces of bright orange card stock cut to 4 1/2" x 6 3/4", or a single piece of orange butcher paper cut to 4 1/2" x 13 1/2"
- 1" x 6 1/2" strip of orange paper or card stock for a beard, and a scrap for the eyebrows
- Light green card stock — 1 sheet for the four leaf clover, 2 strips of 1" x 6 3/4", and one strip of 1 1/2" x 11"
- 4" x 4" square of scrap, light pink or flesh-colored card stock
- 2" x 2" scrap of bright yellow card stock for the buckle
- 1 1/4" sheet of kelly green poster board—2" x 13 1/2" strip, bow, and circular hat brim from pattern.
- Fine point green, red, and blue permanent markers
- Craft glue and hot glue
- Larry the Leprechaun pattern (page 71)

INSTRUCTIONS

1. Measure, cut, and wrap the can with orange card stock.

2. Trace the leprechaun pattern pieces onto the colored papers, and cut them out.

3. Wrap the 1 1/2" x 11" light green paper strip around the base of the can, leaving 1 1/2" area of orange exposed in the front. Glue in position.

4. Use a green marker to mark the detail lines on the kelly green

bow. Use the red and blue markers to mark the facial detail lines on the pink face piece. Glue the orange eyebrow shapes onto the face.

5. Center and glue the bow in front, over the light green base strip. Glue the four leaf clover to the right side of the bow.

6. Snip 3/4" lines at 1/4" increments along one edge of the 1" x 6 1/2" orange strip of paper. *Carefully*, use scissors to curl the very ends of these increments on the beard strip. Hot glue the solid 1/4" edge of the beard strip to the back side of the face paper, curving it around the chin edge of the face. Position and glue the bearded pink face to the front, slightly overlapping in front of the bow.

7. Hat Brim

a. Cut the circular hat pattern from the kelly green poster board. Cut out the solid inner center.

b. Cut along the marked lines around the inside opening, creating 1" tabs. Fold back each of the tabs toward the outer ring of the hat rim. Very gently, slide the circle opening over the top of the can until the circular rim is just covering the forehead of the face. Apply a dot of glue to the back side of each of the tabs, and press the tabs to the can to hold the hat rim in place. Run a line of glue around the outside of the tabs, just above the crease of where the tabs and the rim of the hat meet.

c. Place the 2" x 13 1/2" paper strip over the tabs. Keep the bottom edge of the strip flush with the crease of the tabs and hat rim.

Have the overlapping edges meet at the back of the can.

d. Glue the two light green strips (1" x 6 3/4") just along the bottom edge of the kelly green hat strip to form a band. Glue the yellow buckle in front, on top of the light green band.

When you finish making this whimsical leprechaun, he'll seem to say "Top of the Morning to You!" It's certain that he'll bring that Irish spirit alive on St. Patrick's Day. Fill him full of gold foil-covered chocolate coins, and he becomes his own pot of gold.

Chicks & eggs can

Special tools:

- 1/4" circle hole punch
- Tweezers
- Optional — rubber cement pick up square

Materials:

- 1 clean #10 can with white plastic lid
- 2 sheets of 8 1/2" x 11" pre-printed scrapbook paper or one continuous length 6 3/4" x 20" light blue paper or gift wrap
- 5 yellow chick die cuts with orange beaks and pairs of feet, 5 beaks and 10 feet (I used Pebbles in My Pocket custom die cuts)
- 5 pairs of cracked egg halves (I used Pebbles in My Pocket custom die cuts)
- 2 light green grass border die cuts, 3 darker green grass borders (I used Ellison Educational die cuts)
- 2 colors of flower die cuts (I used Ellison Educational die cuts)
- 2 large white daisies, 4 small white daisies, 2 large pink flowers, 4 small pink flowers
- Scrap of pastel yellow card stock
- Fine point black permanent marker
- Glue stick for paper (I used Aleene's 2 in 1 glue stick)

INSTRUCTIONS

1. Either glue two pieces of scrapbook paper together or use a full length of 6 3/4" x 20" paper. Start placing and arranging the die cuts over the full length of the paper. Try overlapping pieces and adjusting the die cuts in different angles and positions. I started by placing the light green grass borders behind the dark green grass shapes. Then I placed, moved, and rearranged the die cuts around the paper until I achieved a look I was happy with. I used my 1/4" hole punch to create small, yellow circles to glue in the middle of the flower die cuts. Tweezers are a much-appreciated tool when it comes to gluing and placing small paper pieces.

2. Glue the die cut shapes in place. Use a fine point, black marker to make little eye dots on the chicks. I found that a rubber cement pick-up square comes in handy to remove any tacky or smudgy glue spots that might've resulted from the creative process.

3. Wrap and glue the designed paper around the container (or place Velcro squares on the corners so you can change the can with each occasion). Fill the can with Easter goodies.

This delightful container is another useful way to use up those extra die cuts that you thought were so cute, that you just had to have, and then ended up buying a whole handful. Whether or not these exact die cuts are available in your local area, this example will hopefully get your creative juices flowing to help you mimic this design with similar die cuts or fuel your creativity and imagination to use other extra die cuts you might have.

tips & SUGGESTIONS

This can could also be made into an Easter egg pail. Punch or drill holes on each side, and thread #20 gauge craft wire through the holes to make a handle. Cut a 3" x 6" rectangle from a sheet of yellow or blue craft foam. Wrap and glue the foam around the middle of the craft wire to make a hand cushion.

boris the bunny

MATERIALS:

- 1 clean #10 can with white plastic lid
- 1 clean tuna can or chunk chicken can (2 1/4" x 4" diameter)
- 6 3/4" x 20" white butcher paper or gift wrap
- 4" x 13 1/2" long, white butcher paper or gift wrap
- 1 sheet of 8 1/2" x 11" pink card stock
- 3 1/2" diameter white card stock paper circle
- 1 white poster board
- 2, 9" clear plastic-coated wires or plain wire
- 2, 4" long white pipe cleaners (chenille stems)
- 1, 2" diameter white pom pom for tail
- Pink chalk
- Fine point blue and pink permanent markers
- Hot glue and craft glue
- Boris the Bunny pattern (page 72)

INSTRUCTIONS

1. Cut and wrap the 6 3/4" x 20" paper around the #10 can. Glue it in place where the paper overlaps itself.

2. Wrap and cover the tuna can with the 4" x 13 1/2" white paper piece. Fold 1/2" of paper into the interior of the can, and glue it in place. Where the other 3 1/2" of paper overlaps and gathers at the bottom of the can, glue the 3 1/2" diameter white card stock circle over the paper to give it a smooth, finished look.

3. Trace the bunny pattern pieces onto white poster board (ears, feet, and arms) and pink card stock (inner ears, inner feet, and nose), and cut them out.

4. Glue the inner ear and paw pad shapes to the ear and feet shapes. Draw along the outside edge of the arm paws with a pink marker.

5. Bend the pipe cleaners over 1" to create an L-shape. Glue the longest lengths in the center of the back sides of the white ear pieces. Fold the ears at the dotted lines. Position and glue the 1" bent sections to the top of the inverted tuna can (the true bottom of the can).

6. Center and trace the face pattern onto the covered tuna can. Trace and mark the eye dots with a blue marker. Glue the pink heart nose onto the front of the can.

7. Fold the two 9", clear, plastic-coated wires in half, and bend them in a zig-zag fashion for whiskers. Glue the wire whiskers (where they bend in the middle) under the nose.

8. Glue the flat, straight edge of the arms in front and just below the top metal lip on the #10 can. Position and glue the white poster board feet on the front of the can.

9. Center and glue Boris' head (tuna can) to the top of the white plastic lid.

BORIS MAKES A FUN SPRINGTIME DECORATION. YOU CAN FILL HIM FULL OF TREATS, AND PRESENT HIM TO A SPECIAL PERSON IN YOUR LIFE. HE IS GUARANTEED TO BRIGHTEN ANYONE'S SPRING DAY.

faux watering can

Materials:

- 1 clean #10 can
- 3 sheets of 8 1/2" x 11" light weight chip board (cut 2 sheets to 6 3/4" x 10"; cut the third sheet into a 1" x 11" strip for the side handle, spout flange, and sprinkle cap patterns)
- 8" x 3" diameter cone (I used STYROFOAM® brand foam)
- 1 sheet of 8 1/2" x 11" card stock, any color
- Approx. 32" of aluminum foil
- Hot glue
- 1 sheet of 6" x 8" Bristol paper
- 1/4" hole punch
- Watering can pattern (page 73)
- Flourish pattern (page 65)

Instructions

1. Center and trace the flourish design onto the 2 sheets of chip board. This will give you the design on both sides of the can. Tape and seam together the chip board sheets, making a continuous length of 6 3/4" x 20.

2. Trace the design with a beaded line of hot glue. When the raised glue cools and dries, carefully wrap a 7 3/4" x 21" piece of foil over the raised design. Fold the overlapping edges to the back side of the chipboard. Carefully rub the foil in around the design.

3. Wrap your raised foil design around the can, and glue the overlapping edges to each other. Be careful not to glue the chip board design to the can.

4. Cut out the watering can pattern pieces. Cut the spout cover out of both Bristol paper and aluminum

foil. Spot glue around the edges to adhere foil to Bristol paper.

5. Wrap and cover the flange and sprinkle cap with foil. Snip the short lines on the sprinkle cap to create tabs. Using the 1/4" hole punch, punch sprinkle holes in the sprinkle cap.

6. Use the diagram and directions (page 73) to cut the STYROFOAM® cone. Wrap and glue the foil-covered spout arm cover around the cone.

7. Wrap the foil-covered spout flange tightly around the top narrow end of the cone shape of the spout arm. Hot glue the edges where they overlap. Glue the flange in place on the spout arm.

8. Fold the tabs inward on the foil-covered sprinkle cap. Placing

glue along the tabs, position the sprinkle cap inside of the spout flange.

9. For the handle, wrap the 1" x 11" chip board strip with foil. Curl 2 1/2" at the end of the strip. Slide 1" of the other end of the handle down behind and between the cover paper seam and the can. Curve the handle out a little, and glue the handle strip to the can where the 2 1/2" curl begins. Pull the other 1" end out from between the cover paper and can. Apply craft glue to the end of the strip, and replace the end of the strip between the cover paper and the can. *Remember the paper handle is for decoration and will not support the can.*

10. Fill the can with a silk floral bouquet or plant.

From a distance, a person might do a double take. Who would know this watering can is just a decorated coffee can? Filled with silk flowers or plants, it makes a charming centerpiece.

graduate cans

MATERIALS:

- 1 clean #10 can
- 1 piece of 6 3/4" x 11" skin-color paper
- Hair—6 3/4" x 14" paper or two sheets of 8 1/2" x 11"
- Scraps of paper for eyebrows, matching hair color paper
- Scraps of white card stock for eyes and mouth
- 1" black pom pom
- 21, 14" strands of embroidery thread in the color of the graduate's school
- Black poster board—2 1/2" x 20 1/2" for black hatband, 8 1/2" x 8 1/2" for black cap top
- Fine point black permanent marker
- Pink marker or crayon
- Hot glue or craft glue
- Paper glue stick
- Face patterns (page 75)

INSTRUCTIONS

1. Trace your chosen face pattern onto the center of your skin-tone paper. Trace the eyebrows onto the hair-color scrap paper. Trace the eyes and mouth shapes (teeth shape for darker-skinned male) from white card stock.

2. With a black marker, trace the face lines, eyes, and the lip areas on the mouth of the female and lighter-skinned male. Color in the lips with pink.

3. Wrap and glue the 6 3/4" x 11" skin-color paper to the front of the can. Glue the face pieces on.

4. Hair Covering for the Female—With a full sheet of yel-low card stock, cut 1" increment paper strips 1 3/4" up along the 11" length of the paper. Center, wrap, and glue this sheet along the top back side of the can. Cut the other sheet of yellow card stock in half to make two 8 1/2" x 5 1/2" pieces. Cut angular 1" cuts down one side and along the bottom of these pieces. Glue and place these pieces, overlapping 2 1/2", onto the back hair piece on each side. Use scissors to carefully curl the ends upward on the cut strips of paper.

5. For the Male Hair—Fold the 6 3/4" x 14" black paper in half, with ends matched up. Cut and trim along the ends by tapering back at the top (sideburns) and bottom, include cutting an ear area out. Glue the black hair paper along the edges, and wrap it around the back side of the can, bringing the sides toward the front.

6. **Black Cap**—Cut an 8 1/2" x 8 1/2" square and a 2 1/2" x 20 1/2" band from the black poster board. Trace and cut out the cap band center line. Cut 1/2" x 1/2" increments along the top edge of the long black band to make tabs. Wrap the band around the top of the can. Make sure it's slightly bigger than the circumference of the can, so the cap will slide easily on and off. Glue the overlapping edges of the band together. Fold back each of the tabs, and apply glue to the top of the tabs. Center and glue the black square cap top on top of the tabbed band. Glue the pom pom to the top center of the cap.

7. **Tassel**—Cut one strand of embroidery thread in half. Evenly fold the other 20 strands. Tie the bunch together with half of the leftover strand, 3/4" down from top, folded-over section. Thread the other half of the strand through the loop at the top of the bunch (created by doubling over the strands). Attach the tassel to the pom pom at the top of the cap.

tips ― SUGGESTIONS

On the darker-skinned male, I painted the eyes and teeth white .

THESE GIFT CONTAINERS SHOW THE THRILL OF ACHIEVEMENT. WITH YOUR CREATIVE LICENSE AND THE PATTERNS PROVIDED, YOU CAN EASILY CHANGE THE PAPER HAIR COLOR AND SKIN TONE TO MATCH (AS CLOSELY AS POSSIBLE) YOUR INTENDED GRADUATE. PLACE A GIFT ITEM INSIDE OR LOOSELY CRUMPLE TWENTY-FIVE OR FIFTY DOLLAR BILLS. WHAT GRADUATE WOULDN'T BE PLEASED AND GRATEFUL FOR SUCH A GIFT?

bridal shower wedding cake decoration

From a distance, shower party guests would never know this wedding cake was created without the heat and toil of the kitchen. This project is a great opportunity to experiment and decorate a wedding cake without the worry of the cake collapsing.

MATERIALS:

- 3 white nesting craft tins or 3 cookie tins of different sizes
- Paint primer and white spray paint (I used Krylon Primer and interior/exterior flat white #1502)
- 1, 12" white, 16-gauge, cloth-wrapped, wire
- 2, 12" pieces of white florist wire
- 4 1/2 to 5 yards of decorative white trim (I used Wrights 3/8" white, twisted satin cord with pearls)
- 15" of 1/4" white, iridescent, pearl curling ribbon
- Silk floral picks of your choice (I used 3 wine color Silken Sweet William x2 by Regency International)
- 3 floral spray picks (I used wine-color pussy willow buds on sage green wire)
- 100+ 1/8" diameter round white pearl beads, 25 rice-shaped, 3 teardrop (I used Bits & Pieces mixed pearls #1441-05 by Cousin Corporation of America)
- Hot glue
- 12" diameter cardboard circle
- Gold spray paint (I used Krylon metallic gold)
- Cake topper pattern (page 77)

INSTRUCTIONS

1. If you are using recycled tins, separate lids from the tins. Before spray painting on metal, sand the surfaces with fine steel wool, wipe clean, coat with paint primer, and then apply spray paint on the lids and tins. Follow the painting instructions on page 8 to paint the tins white. Set aside to dry.

2. Pull off clusters of the silk, Sweet William flowers and glue a small 1/8" diameter pearl bead in the center of each one. Wrap, cut, and glue lengths of the white, twisted satin cord around the base and lid rims of each of the three tins. Measure lengths of the pussy willow wire, and attach them together by twisting their wire ends. In a wave fashion, wrap the wires around the tins. Glue four single flowers, equally distanced around the lids of the bottom and middle tins.

3. Heart-Shaped Cake Topper (diagram is actual size) — Bend the 16-gauge wire into a heart shape. Glue the white satin cord to both sides of the heart. Glue 15" of 1/4" white, iridescent, pearl curling ribbon around the outer exposed wire of the heart. Set aside.

4. Cut both of the 12" white florist wires in half. Take the four wires, and twist and fold them in the middle to create a spray of eight 3" wires. Use one of the wires to wrap and secure the group of wires at the base of the group, leaving about 2" of wire hanging at the base. Thread pearl beads onto each of the 7 wires, starting with three rice shaped beads, then three beads (slightly larger than 1/8"), then five 1/8" diameter beads, and then three beads (slightly smaller than 1/8"). Top the three center wires with a teardrop-shaped bead, and hot glue one of the beads (slightly smaller than 1/8") at the very end. Top the four outer wires with four rice-shaped beads, and hot glue one of the beads (slightly smaller than 1/8") at the very end.

5. Take the 2" of extra wire at the base of the beaded pearl spray, and wrap the spray to the base of the heart shaped wire.

6. Center the heart, and hot glue it on top of the smallest tin. Position and glue four clusters of the Sweet William flowers around the base of the cake topper.

7. Stack the tins and glue them together.

8. As a finishing touch, spray paint a cardboard circle (that is 4" larger in diameter than the diameter of your bottom tin) gold or silver. In this case, the circle is 12" in diameter. Glue silk leaves and six bunches of three flowers each around the cardboard circle in a wreath fashion.

tips & SUGGESTIONS

If you don't glue the cans to one another, they can be separated to become decorative storage tins on a vanity top. Or ...

Decorate the tins with fresh flowers.

1. Make sure the tins don't leak when they're filled with water.

2. Paint and decorate the outsides of the tins.

3. Cut floral oasis blocks to fit inside the tins, forming a ring toward the outside edges.

4. Cut three white disposable foam plates into circles with the same interior diameters as the tins.

5. Fill the tins 3/4 full with water, and put in any floral preservative treatment, if you wish. Place the matching diameter white foam plate on top of the appropriate tin, and stack the tins on top of each other.

6. Stick the fresh floral stems through the white foam, around and on top of the tins. Focus the decorative floral emphasis at the very top.

Wedding reception candleholders

MATERIALS:

- 1 clean 3.5 oz. potato chip canister
- 1 clean 2 oz. potato chip canister
- White spray paint (I used Krylon interior/exterior flat white #1502)
- 2, 3 1/2" or 4" diameter plastic doll plates, small saucers, or candle plate shields
- 4, 10" pieces of Wrights 3/8" white, twisted satin cord with pearls
- 1 pearl berries floral pick (I used UPC 76090 by Darice)
- Green florist tape
- 1 sheet of 8 1/2" x 11" pure white mulberry paper cut into: 5 1/4" x 10" and 3 1/4" x 10"
- Thick craft glue and hot glue (I used The Ultimate Crafter's Pick by API)

INSTRUCTIONS

1. Remove plastic lids from the potato chip canisters, and save them for another use. Center and glue (thick craft glue) the plastic doll plates to the top rims of the two canisters. Set them aside, and allow to dry.

2. Following the painting instructions on page 8, spray the canisters with the white spray paint.

3. Wrap and glue the 5 1/4" by 10" piece of white mulberry paper around the 3.5 oz. canisters. Wrap and glue the other piece of white paper around the 2 oz. canister.

4. Wrap and glue (with hot glue) a length of satin cord around the top and bottom of each of the canisters.

5. Select a couple of stems with one to two leaves and a cluster of

These candleholders hold 3" diameter candles and can be decorated to match the bride and groom's wedding colors and floral choices. Save up several potato chip canisters of different sizes, decorate them, and place a grouping of candleholders at each guest table at the reception.

pearl berries. You may need to wrap the ends of the stems with green floral tape to hide any exposed wires. Bend and coil the stem ends, and glue them to the front of the canisters. The wedding party will never know the candleholders are from recycled containers.

Mini watering cans

Special tools:

- 1/8" hole punch and 1/4" hole punch
- Decorative edged scissors— short wavy cut
- Novelty shape paper punches— large flower, small flower, heart, large circle

Materials:

- Clean 3" x 2 5/8" diameter metal cans (I used 8 oz. tomato sauce cans)
- 1 sheet of 8 1/2"x 11" card stock for each can, any color
- Scraps of brightly-colored paper to coordinate with punched designs
- Stickers for the white watering can
- Extra fine tip black marker
- Hot glue and craft glue
- Mini watering can patterns (page 74)

Instructions

1. Photocopy the mini watering can patterns onto a sheet of colored card stock.

2. Cut out the pattern pieces. Be sure to cut on the inside of the black pattern outlines, so the black lines will not be seen on the paper.

3. Wrap the 9" cover strip around the can, and glue the overlapping edges to each other. Don't glue the paper to the can.

4. Snip the short lines on the spill cover and sprinkle cap to create tabs. Use the 1/8" hole punch to punch sprinkle holes in the sprinkle cap piece.

5. Decorating the Can— This step is completely left up to you, whether you decide to apply decorative stickers, rub on transfers, paint, or cut and use paper punch designs to embellish the can.

6. Form the spout arm piece into a cone shape, overlapping the edges about 1/4". Glue the edges in place with hot glue.

7. Wrap the spout flange tightly around the top narrow end of the spout arm. Hot glue the edges where they overlap. Glue the flange in place on the spout arm.

8. On the sprinkle cap, fold the tabs inward. Place glue on the tabs, and position the sprinkle cap inside of the flange.

9. On the spill cover, fold the tabs inward. Apply hot glue along the tabs, and center the spill cover inside the rim of the can.

10. Just behind the spill cover, glue the ends of the top handle to the opposite sides of the interior of the can.

11. Curl 2 1/2" at one end of the side handle strip. At the other end of the handle strip, slide 1 3/4" between the cover paper seam and the can. Curve the handle out a little, and glue the curled end of the handle strip near the bottom of the can. Pull the other end out from between the cover paper and can. Apply craft glue at the end of the strip, and replace it between the cover paper and can. *The paper handles are for decoration only and will not support the can.*

These decorative, little watering cans are perfect as party favors for a springtime party. Decorate them any way you wish, and fill them with small candies and mints. They also make for a charming springtime shelf decoration.

American flag can

Special tool needed:

- 1/2" star punch

Materials:

- 1 clean #10 can
- 8 3/4" x 20" piece of brown paper shopping bag, brown craft paper, or white gift wrap
- 1 sheet of 8 1/2" x 11" card stock in beige, brick red, and indigo blue
- Paper glue or thick craft glue
- Flag and star patterns (page 76)

Instructions

1. Wrap the paper around the can, and glue the overlapping edges into the interior of the can and onto the bottom.

2. Trace the various shapes of the flag and star designs onto the card stock, and cut the shapes out (stripes—red; flag and star left corner—blue; star and star punches—beige).

3. Position and glue the colored pieces onto the front of the can.

Teacher Project

Photocopy pattern pieces onto beige card stock. Have students color in the stripes and stars, or punch blue and red paper circles and yellow stars to glue onto the stripes and star areas. Cover cans with paper bags, and have the students glue their flag and star designs onto the front.

Fill this container with homemade goodies. It makes a wonderful gift of gratitude and appreciation to give to a veteran. Or, fill it with cookies or candies, and bring it to a Fourth of July picnic. It becomes a very nice display as a simple patriotic decoration.

tips & Suggestions

This design could easily be painted on colored card stock and then wrapped around the can.

freedom rockets decoration

This PROJECT MAKES A SHOWY, PATRIOTIC, AMERICAN
CENTERPIECE. READ ON TO FIND OUT WHICH RECYCLED ITEMS
WERE USED TO CREATE THIS CENTERPIECE.

For Freedom Rockets:
- White paper beverage cups in three sizes (you could spray paint fast food cups)
- 3 cardboard toilet paper tubes
- 2 pieces of 8 1/2" x 11" metallic blue foil card stock
- 1 piece of 8 1/2" x 11" metallic red foil card stock
- 6 strips of red ribbon or red paper
- 1/2" silver, red, and blue foil stars
- 6, 12" bamboo shish-ka-bob skewers
- Red and blue permanent markers or paint
- Spool kegs of curling ribbon — metallic red, blue, and silver and plain white
- Hot glue and thick craft glue
- Rocket caps pattern (page 78)

INSTRUCTIONS

Uncle Sam Hat Rocket Holder:

1. Wrap the can with the white paper. Overlap and glue excess paper into the interior of the can.

2. **Hat Rim**—Measure, mark, and cut a 6 1/4" diameter circle out of blue foil card stock. Measure and mark 3 1/2" and 4" circles in the center of this circle. Cut out the inner 3 1/2" circle. Snip 1" increments from the center of the 3 1/2" circle to the 4" marked circle. Continue around the inside opening, clipping these increments to create 1/4" high x 1" wide tabs. Fold each of the tabs toward the outer ring of the hat rim. Very gently slide the circle opening over the top of the can and down until the circular rim is level with the bottom rim of the can. Apply a

Special tool needed:
- 1/2" star punch

Materials:

For Uncle Sam Hat Rocket Holder:
- 1 clean 1lb. (pumpkin or pie filling) can—4 3/4" x 4" diameter
- 7 1/2" x 13 1/2" piece of white butcher paper or gift wrap
- 11 strips of 3/4" x 5" red ribbon or red paper
- 1 piece of 8 1/2" x 11" metallic blue foil card stock—cut a 1 3/4" x 11" strip and a 1 3/4" x 2 1/2" extension strip; use clear tape on the back edge to attach the two, creating a continuous 1 3/4" x 13" band
- White, plastic foam cylinder or stack disks—cut 3 1/2" x 3 3/4" diameter to fit in can

dot of glue to the back side of each of the tabs, and press the tabs to the can to hold the hat rim in place.

3. Place and glue the red strips 1 1/2" up from the bottom of the can and 3/8" apart around the can. Fold the top portions of the ribbons over, and glue them down into the interior of the can.

4. Punch 11 stars along one edge of the blue foil strip. Flip the strip over, and punch 11 stars staggered between each of the previously punched stars running along the other edge. Wrap and glue the star-punched foil strip around the can, covering the edges of the ribbon and tabs from the hat rim.

5. Place the plastic foam into the can.

Freedom Rockets:

1. Decorate the white paper cups with foil star stickers and red ribbon stripes. The largest cup (5" tall) was glued with six strips of 3/4" x 5 1/2" red ribbon, vertically around the cup.

2. Cut the red foil sheet into two 4 1/2" x 5 1/2" pieces and one 4" x 5 1/2" piece. Wrap and glue the red foil pieces around the toilet paper tubes. One tube will need to be cut down for the 4" x 5 1/2" red foil piece.

3. Using the rocket caps patterns, trace and cut three blue foil caps for paper cups and three foil caps for the toilet paper tubes. Overlap the blue foil rocket cap edges to form a conical peak. Glue the overlapping edges in place with hot glue. Apply hot glue or craft glue along the top lip of the cups and red tubes. Center and place the conical-shaped rocket caps on top of the containers.

4. Ribbon rocket smoke — Cut seven strands of red, blue, and silver, and nine strands of white curling ribbon at 18"–25" in length. For the largest cup, gather 14 strands — three of red, blue, and silver, and five of white, in a bunch. For the other two cups, gather 8 strands, two of each color. Tie a knot in the middle of each of the bunches. Curl the ribbons to various lengths and tightnesses. Poke a small hole in the bottom center of each of the white rockets (cups). Carefully push the knotted bunches of curling ribbon through the hole.

5. Color or paint over three bamboo skewers with the red marker, and the other three with the blue marker. Hot glue the skewers to the underside and against the rims of the cups and red tubes.

6. Arrange and stick the rockets into the foam insert of the Uncle Sam hat holder.

TEACHER PROJECT

bug jars

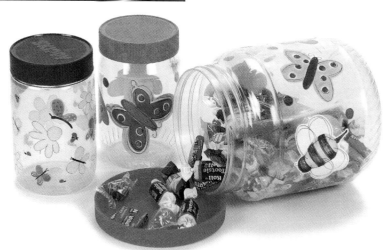

At first glance, these look like they are hand painted glass jars. Fill them with candies, small objects, marbles, and beads, or make them into great bug housing jars (just be sure to pound a few holes in the lid to give air to your new pets).

MATERIALS:

- 2 or 3 clean, plastic peanut butter jars with bright-colored lids
- Stickers — Clear background stickers give the look that you've actually hand painted right on the jar. (I used Bitty Stickers, Posie Accents Item #42-0788 designed by Kathy Griffiths, and Provo Craft and Me & My BIG ideas Bug Stickers item # SMR–03)

INSTRUCTIONS

1. Clean out the peanut jars, and remove any sticky adhesive left over from the label.

2. Select, arrange, and place the stickers in a pattern all around the jars.

3. Fill the jar with your goodies of choice. Personally, I prefer the non-crawling goodies.

dragonfly gift container

MATERIALS:

- 1 oatmeal canister with a plastic lid
- Silver, iridescent mini keg spool of 1/8" curling ribbon
- 1 yard of clear, iridescent AM Paper Twist (Item # 60201 by American Twisting Company)
- 4 to five gold metallic tinsel pipe cleaners (chenille stems)
- 2 silver metallic tinsel pipe cleaners (chenille stems)
- Your choice of gift wrap to cut and wrap around your canister (I used Hallmark Expressions)
- 1 metal or bamboo skewer
- Hot glue or thick craft glue
- Wings pattern (page 77)

INSTRUCTIONS

1. Measure, cut, wrap, and glue the gift wrap around the canister.

2. Open and flatten out the clear paper twist. Using the wings pattern, cut out two sets of wings for each of the dragonflies. (I found that it was easier to fold the paper twist a couple times to create four, or up to eight layers, and cut the wing sets all at once.)

3. Assemble dragonfly wings onto the metallic pipe cleaners.

a. Bend pipe cleaner end over 1 1/2" and form a heart shape at the end.

b. Twist pipe cleaner around skewer four times tightly and close together. Slide skewer out.

c. Place the middle of the first set of wings in between the third and fourth coil. Press the coils tightly together.

d. Twist the pipe cleaner around the skewer three times tightly and close together. Slide the skewer out.

This container is great for the friend who is crazy about dragonflies. It makes a very fun and unique birthday or special gift box.

e. Place the middle of the second set of wings in between the last coil. Press the coils tightly together.

f. Continue twisting and coiling the pipe cleaner down 3" on the skewer, slide skewer out.

4. Position and glue the dragonflies anywhere you desire. Twist and wrap a coiled silver pipe cleaner around a couple of dragonflies, and glue the ends of the silver pipe cleaners to the top of the container lid to give the illusion of the dragonflies suspended in flight.

5. Cut several long strands of 1/8" curling ribbon. Curl and create a bow for the top of the lid.

beverage cup birdhouses

Special Tools Needed:

- Foam brushes, sizes 1", 2", and 3" (I used Loew-Cornell Foam brush set #1130)

Materials:

- Your choice of different sized and shaped fast food beverage cups and juice, milk, and cracker cartons
- 1/8" wooden dowels, cut to 13 1/4", 14 3/4", and 18"
- Sheets of preprinted scrapbook paper and 5" x 7" die cut frame (I used Scrap in a Snap)
- Stickers (I used Doodle bugs designs by Cynthea Sandoval, provided by Scrap in Snap)
- Acrylic Paints (I used Delta Ceramcoat paints)
  - Yellow acrylic paint—custard #2448
  - Bright Blue acrylic paint—ocean reef blue #2074
  - White acrylic paint—white #2505
  - Green acrylic paint—kelly green #2052
  (If you choose to use acrylic paints, you might consider applying an acrylic sealer as a final coat to protect the painted surface from chipping or peeling.)
- Craft knife
- Thick, heavy duty cardboard box—4 1/2" x 9 1/4" x 4 1/4"
- Hot glue
- Decorative paper cutting scissors (I used Fiskars Paper Edgers, Regular, Seagull)
- Handful of shredded tissue, Spanish moss, or excelsior for nesting material

These birdhouses are simple and charming decorations to display. Recreate these birdhouses, or use colorful, printed scrapbook, card stock papers and stickers to create your own.

INSTRUCTIONS

1. Use a 2" foam brush to paint the cups and cartons in your choice of colors. Remember to apply several thin, even coats to completely cover any printed graphics on the containers. Allow each coat to dry completely between applications.

2. Paint the wooden dowels with blue. At this time, you could also be applying coats of green paint to completely cover your cardboard box. When the box is covered and dry, use the 1" foam brush to paint white fence lines around the box.

3. To make the door openings, mark small circles on the fronts of the cup and cartons, and cut the circles out with a craft knife. Or, punch or cut out small black circles, then glue the circles to the fronts of the cups, indicating the door openings.

4. When making the conical roofs, you will need to measure and cut a circle 2"–2 3/4" larger in diameter than that of the top opening of the cup. Measure your square or rectangular roof pieces 1/4"–1/2" larger than the actual dimension of the square and rectangular cartons, so you will have an nice overhang. Measure and mark each roof piece according to your chosen cups and cartons.

5. Cut out the circle roofs. If you have some fun, decorative-edge scissors, cut your roofs out with these. They add a nice touch. Remember to go slowly, and realign the cutting edge to achieve a continued, even-patterned edge.

6. To shape the conical roofs, mark the exact center point of the diameter of the circles. Cut a straight line from the outer edge of the roof circles to the center point of the circles. Overlap the cut edges to form a cone to a desired conical peak. Glue the overlapping edges with hot glue.

7. Apply hot glue or craft glue along the top rim of the cups. Center and place the conical-shaped roofs on top of the containers.

8. Fold the printed die cut frame, center it, and glue it to the top of the square or rectangle carton birdhouse.

9. Poke a center hole in the bottom of the cups and carton, by making a small X with a craft knife. Next place a dot of glue over the cut X mark, and push one end of a painted dowel through the glue and up into the cup. Set aside to dry. Repeat this step on all the birdhouses.

10. Decide where you would like the birdhouse dowels to come out of your green fence box base. Make a small X with a craft knife, place a dot of glue on the X, and push the dowel perches down through the box base.

11. Apply stickers to the outside of the birdhouses, any way you wish. If you're feeling creative and would like to paint your own original artwork, by all means fire away.

12. Stuff small amounts of shredded tissue, Spanish moss, or excelsior into the birdhouse openings as nesting material.

tips & SUGGESTIONS

Use small, decorative paper cups, and apply the above instructions to your cups, minus the painting. Use either a dowel or bamboo skewer as the birdhouse support. These small, single birdhouses make darling plant pokes.

Nursery clown

MATERIALS:

- 1 clean 6 oz. potato chip canister with plastic lid
- Brand new and full—Renuzit LongLast Adjustable Air Freshener
- 1 sheet of 8 1/2" x 11" preprinted scrapbook paper or gift wrap paper (I used Baby Sleep Tight by Rebecca Carter, Provo Craft)
- 1/2 sheet of 8 1/2" x 11" pastel yellow card stock or felt
- 21" pastel yellow 1/2" wide satin ribbon
- 10" pastel blue 3/4" wide satin ribbon
- 11" pastel yellow satin baby blanket binding trim (or 2" wide satin ribbon, needle, and yellow thread)
- 2 baby blue pipe cleaners (chenille stems)
- 3, 1" baby blue pom poms
- 1, 1" yellow and one 10mm yellow pom pom
- Fine point blue and yellow permanent markers
- Elmer's 3D washable Sparkle Glitter Paint Pens with blue and yellow in the pack
- Hot glue gun or craft glue
- Clown face and mittens patterns (page 77)

INSTRUCTIONS

1. Wrap the sheet of printed paper around the potato chip canister. Push the edge of the paper right up to the rim at the top, and glue in place. The original covering of the canister will show at the bottom. If it matches with your choice of paper, great! If not, you might want to cut a strip of coordinating paper or ribbon (11" pastel yellow 1/2" wide satin ribbon) to wrap and cover the exposed bottom area of the canister.

2. Place and glue the yellow 10mm and two 1" blue pom poms in a row, centered in front. Glue the remaining pom poms to the top of the air freshener.

3. Trace the face pattern onto the bottom portion of the air freshener, and color the eye dots with blue, the nose oval with yellow, and the smile line with blue fine point marker. There is a very slight raised design on the upper portion of the air freshener container. (I colored these designs with the blue and yellow sparkle glitter paint pens, as accents, and I added little swirl designs with the sparkle pens on the decorative paper covering the canister.)

4. Wrap and glue the blue satin ribbon around the extended rim portion where the air freshener is opened. Apply 10" of the pale yellow ribbon on top of the blue.

5. Measure and cut a 2 3/4" diameter circle out of the yellow card stock. Trace and cut 4 mittens out of the yellow paper or felt. Coil the baby blue pipe cleaners around a pencil to create the coil arms, and glue two yellow mittens back-to-back over one end of each of the coiled pipe cleaner arms. Center and glue the other ends of the arms to the top of the plastic canister lid. Glue the yellow paper circle on top of the glued ends of the pipe cleaner arms on the plastic lid.

6. To create the neck ruffle, gather stitch along one edge of the yellow satin ribbon. If you have the baby blanket trim, you can eliminate the stitching and gathering.

This cute decoration and gift container is a sweet little present to give to a new mother and babe. Use a brand new Renuzit Air freshener container for the head. Fill the canister with cotton balls, Q-tips, or any other small baby essential.

Glue the ruffled ribbon to the top and along the outside edge of the yellow, paper-covered plastic lid.

7. Finish by gluing the bottom of the air freshener on top of the lid. Fill the canister with treats, and place the clown head lid back on.

birthday clown

Materials:

- 6 oz. red potato chip canister with plastic lid
- Empty air freshener container (I used Renuzit LongLast adjustable air freshener)
- 1 sheet of 8 1/2" x 11" preprinted scrapbook paper (I used Francis Meyer, Inc.)
- 1/2 sheet of 8 1/2" x 11" red card stock or red felt
  - Optional: 1/2" x 11" wide ribbon or colored paper to cover exposed bottom of canister
- 10" of red 1/2" wide satin ribbon
- 11" of royal blue 2" wide satin ribbon
- A needle and blue thread
- 2 blue metallic pipe cleaners (chenille stems)
- 1, 1" blue pom pom
- 1, 1" red pom pom
- 1, 1" green pom pom
- 4" of 2" wide bright yellow ribbon (I used a salvaged bow from a broken hair barrette)
- Fine point blue, red, green, yellow, and black permanent markers
- Hot glue or craft glue
- Clown face and mittens patterns (page 77)

Instructions

1. Wrap the printed paper around the potato chip canister. Push the edge of the paper right up to the rim at the top, and glue it in place. The original covering of the canister will show at the bottom. If it matches with your choice of paper, great! If not, you might want to wrap a strip of coordinating paper or ribbon around the exposed bottom area of the canister.

2. Tie or make a bow out of the yellow ribbon, center it, and glue it toward the top of the canister. Place the green and blue pom poms in a row, just below the yellow bow, and glue them in place. Glue the red pom pom to the top of the air freshener.

3. Trace the face pattern onto the bottom portion of air freshener, and color the eye dots with blue, the nose oval with red, and the smile line with black, fine point markers. There is a very slight raised design on the upper portion of the air freshener container. I colored it in with the red, blue, yellow, and green markers as accents.

4. Wrap and glue the 10" x 1/2" red satin ribbon around the extended rim portion, where the air freshener is opened.

5. Measure and cut a 2 3/4" diameter circle out of the red card stock. Trace and cut 4 mittens out of the red paper or felt. Coil the blue metallic pipe cleaners around a pencil to create the coil arms, and glue two red mittens back-to-back over one end of each of the coiled pipe cleaner arms. Center and glue the other ends of the arms to the top of the plastic canister lid. Place the red paper circle on top of the glued ends of the pipe cleaner arms on the plastic lid, and glue it in place.

6. To create the neck ruffle, gather stitch along one edge of the blue satin ribbon. Glue the ruffled ribbon to the top and along the outside edge of the red, covered plastic lid.

This canister makes a fun birthday decoration. Save up several used air freshener containers and potato chip canisters through the year, and you will be able to make enough clown party favors to give out to party guests. Fill them with candy and small dime store toys.

7. Finish by centering the bottom of the air freshener on top of the lid and gluing it down. Fill the canister with treats, and place the clown head lid back on.

INTERMEDIATE

Sammy scarecrow

MATERIALS:

- 1 clean #10 can
- 6 3/4" x 20" piece cut from a brown paper bag or craft paper, or two sheets of 6 3/4" x 10" light brown card stock
- 2 sheets of 8 1/2" x 11" autumn yellow construction paper or card stock
- 1 sheet of 12" x 12" rust brown poster board for hat brim
- 1" x 20" plaid ribbon in autumn colors
- Small and medium silk sun-flowers with two leaves, or any small autumn decoration pick
- Fine point black permanent marker
- Hot glue gun and glue or craft glue
- Paper glue stick
- Orange and autumn red scraps of paper
- Cheeks and nose pattern

INSTRUCTIONS

1. Trace the face pattern (next page) onto the center of the brown paper. Trace and cut nose (orange) and cheek circles (red) from colored scraps of paper. Glue cheeks and nose in place on face paper. With black marker, color over the traced face lines.

2. Cut two strips, 2" x 10", from the autumn yellow paper. Snip 1" crooked and wavy cuts along the length of the yellow strips. Vary

Sam will provide a warm and welcome feeling to the autumn season. Place an arrangement of autumn leaves and flowers or a plant inside. He makes a darling centerpiece.

the increments from 1/4" to 1/2" to create the look of loose straw.

3. Wrap and glue the solid, uncut 1" edge of the yellow strips around the bottom 1" of the metal

can. Leave the 1" wavy straw fringe hanging over the bottom of the can.

4. Wrap and glue the brown paper around the can and over the top of the glued yellow portion at the bottom of the can. Gently fold the straw fringe upward and toward the can, so it will be level and sticking out when the can is placed on a surface.

5. Straw Hair — Taking the remainder of the yellow paper, cut 5 1/2" x 11", 5 1/2" x 4", and 3" x 11" strips. Cut crooked and wavy cuts, varying the increments from 1/4", 1/2", and just up to 1" from the other edge. Leave a solid 1" border along the length of the yellow strips to create the look of loose straw hair. Wrap and glue the solid uncut 1" edge of the 5 1/2" x 11" yellow strip around the top edge of the back side of the can. Place and glue the 5 1/2" x 4" strip, overlapping 1/2" at one end of the previous strip. Leave the

wavy, straw hair hanging down along the sides of the can.

6. Straw Bangs — Wrap and glue the solid, uncut 1" edge of the 3" x 11" yellow strip around the top edge and in the front of the can, overlapping the other straw-like paper pieces on both sides. Using a pencil or scissors, carefully curl the paper hair strips into loose and tight curls.

7. Floppy Hat Rim — Cut an <u>uneven</u> edge circle, 11 1/2" diameter, from the rust brown poster board. Mark a 6" diameter circle in the center of the 11 1/2" circle. Mark and cut out a circle of 4" diameter in the center of the 6" circle. Clip 1" tabs from the center of the 4" circle to the 6" marked

diameter line. Fold back each of the tabs toward the outer ring of the hat rim. Very gently slide the circle opening over the top of the can, until the circle rim is just far enough down that the top edges of the tabs line up with top edge of the can. Apply a dot of glue to the back side of each of the tabs and press them to the can to hold the hat rim in place.

8. Center, wrap, and glue the plaid ribbon or paper around the hat area covering the tabs.

9. Glue the sunflowers and leaves or decoration/pick in front of the hat on the plaid ribbon.

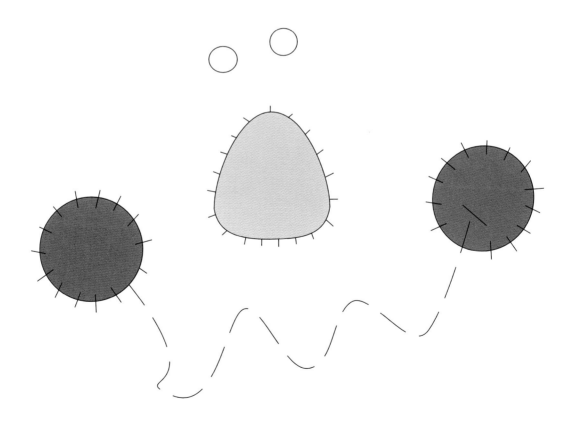

frankie

 **TEACHER PROJECT** By photocopying the pattern to 63% of normal size, the project then fits a smaller, recycled 1 lb. pie filling, large pineapple, or small powdered hot cocoa can, which may be more accessible for the student to bring from home.

MATERIALS:

- 1 clean #10 can
- 2 plastic toothpaste lids, salad bottle lids, or whatever you think resembles bolts
- Silver spray paint (I used Krylon Metallic silver paint.)
- 6 3/4" x 22" olive green paper (I used leftover textured crepe paper gift wrap that I've had for years)
- 6 3/4" x 20" black butcher or construction paper
- White card stock paper
- Purple card stock paper
- Fine point black marker
- Hot glue and thick craft glue
- Face pattern (page 81)

HEY, FRANKIE'S NOT A MONSTER. HE MEANS WELL; HE JUST CAN'T SPEAK UP FOR HIMSELF. FILL HIM FULL OF TREATS AND GIVE HIM TO YOUR FAVORITE HALLOWEEN GOBLIN. HE'LL BE SURE TO EXPRESS A jovial "HAPPY HALLOWEEN."

INSTRUCTIONS

1. Spray the plastic lids with a couple of coats of silver paint. Allow them to dry thoroughly.

2. Trim 2" off the end of the 6 3/4" x 22" olive green paper. Use this 2" strip to trace and cut out the brow pattern piece.

3. Center and trace the hairline portion of the pattern to the black paper. Continue the jagged hairline out along the bottom to both ends of the paper, and cut out. Using the leftover black paper scrap, trace the mouth and eyebrow shapes, and cut them out.

4. Cut the background eye shape and single tooth from a scrap of white card stock.

5. Trace and cut the half oval eyelid shapes from the purple paper.

6. Wrap and glue the 6 3/4" x 20" green paper piece around the can.

7. Leaving a 1/2" overhanging at the top edge of the can, wrap the black paper hair piece around the can. Glue it down where the paper overlaps itself. Fold the overlapping portion into the interior of the can, and glue it down.

8. Using the black marker, color and outline the background eye shape and pupils. Glue the half oval purple eyelid shapes on top of the outlined eye shape. Glue the eye shape about 3 1/4" down from the top and center of the front of the can.

9. Glue the black paper mouth shape below the eyes. Glue the white tooth on the mouth. You could also mark a few scar stitches on his face.

10. Snip the short lines along the top of the green brow pattern piece. Fold these tabs toward the back. Position the brow to slightly overlap the purple eyelids, and hot glue the tabs to the can. Glue the two black eye brows to the top of the brow.

11. With craft glue, glue the bolts to each side of the can.

BEGINNER

Mr. batty

● TEACHER PROJECT

MATERIALS:

- 6 oz. clean, metal mandarin orange cans or small tomato sauce cans
- 3 1/4" x 11" black construction or butcher paper
- 6" x 6" black poster board
- Scraps of red, purple, and white card stock
- Fine point black marker
- Mr. Batty pattern (page 82)

INSTRUCTIONS

1. Wrap and glue the black paper piece around the can.

2. Trace Mr. Batty's body onto the black poster board, and cut it out. Trace and cut out the eye and mouth pieces from the scraps of paper (inner eye—white; outer eye—purple; mouth—red).

3. Glue the purple eye piece on the poster board body of Batty. Glue the white eye piece on top of the purple piece. Use the black marker to outline the white eyes and draw two dots for the pupils.

4. Glue the red mouth piece on. Glue the back side of Batty's body to the can, over the paper seam. Let the glue dry. He's ready to fill up with treats and fly away.

MR. BATTY IS SUPER EASY AND QUICK TO MAKE. FILL HIM FULL OF HALLOWEEN CANDY AND AWAY HE'LL FLY OUT THE DOOR AS A GREAT HALLOWEEN PARTY FAVOR.

Count fangs

He'll vant to suck up all your candy and goodies. He and Mr. Batty would make a whimsical pair, and they certainly won't give anyone too much of a scare.

Materials:

- 1 clean #10 can
- 2 sheets of 8 1/2" x 11" purple-colored card stock
- 5 3/4" x 20" piece of black butcher or construction paper for the hair piece
- 1 1/2" x 20" piece of black butcher or construction paper collar band for the mouth and eyebrow pattern pieces
- 1/2 sheet of black poster board
- 13" x 16" piece of red foil gift wrap
- Scrap of white card stock paper
- Scrap of red and gold foil card stock or paper
- Fine point permanent black marker
- Hot glue and thick craft glue
- Count Fangs pattern (pages 79–80)

Instructions

1. Trim the purple card stock sheets to 6 1/2" x 10". Use the left-over 2" x 11" strip to trace and cut out the two ear pattern pieces. Set ears aside. Wrap and glue the two purple card stock pieces around your can.

2. Center the hairline portion of the face pattern on the 5 3/4" x 20" black paper, and trace it. Continue the hairline along the bottom and out to both ends of the paper, and cut out. Using the leftover black paper scrap, trace and cut out mouth and eyebrows. Trace and cut out the eye shape from a scrap of white card stock. Trace the multi-pointed star (gold) and gem (red) patterns onto the back side of the foil card stock scraps, and cut them out.

3. Using the black marker, color and outline the eyes and pupils. Draw a forward and backward 'S' on the purple ear pieces.

4. Wrap the black, hairline piece around the can, and glue where paper overlaps itself. Leaving a 1 1/2" over hang at the top edge of the can, fold and glue this overlapping portion down into the interior of the can.

5. Glue the eye shape, eyebrows, and mouth onto the front of the can.

6. Wrap the 1 1/2" x 20" black collar band around the base of can, with collar ends meeting in the front. Make diagonal cuts 3" long on both ends, for the impression of a V-neck collar. Glue in place.

7. Fold tabs over on the purple ears, apply glue to tabs, apply ears on each side of the can.

8. Using the cape pattern pieces, trace and create a full cape pattern piece out of scrap paper or news paper. Use this full cape pattern to trace and cut out two cape pieces, one from the black poster board, and the other from 13" x 16" red foil gift wrap.

9. Fold the edges of the red foil cape piece in 1/4" all around the front sides and across the top. Glue the underside of the red foil piece to the top of the black, poster board cape piece (giving the impression of a cape with red lining). Wrap the black cape (with red foil facing inside) around the base of the can, over the black collar area. Hot glue the two pointed tips of the cape directly in the front of the can, under the mouth.

10. Glue the small, red, foil gem piece on top of the gold foil multi-star. Glue the star over the point where the cape tips were glued in front. Fill the Count's head with candy and sweets.

Witchy poo

Special Tools Needed:

- Zigzag, wavy, or deckle edged scissors

Materials:

- 1 clean #10 can
- 3 sheets of 8 1/2" x 11" light green construction paper or butcher paper
- 1/2 sheet of white card stock paper
- 2 sheets of 8 1/2" x 11" orange construction paper or card stock
- 1/2 sheet of 8 1/2" x 11" bright yellow construction paper or card stock
- Funky yellow die cuts
- 9" diameter circle from black poster board for hat brim
- 2 1/2" x 20" black butcher paper
- 17" by 17" quarter circle cut from black butcher paper
- Fine point black permanent marker
- Hot glue
- Paper glue stick
- Face pattern (page 83)

Instructions

1. Trace the face pattern pieces onto the appropriate colored papers, and cut them out.

2. Wrap the green paper around the can. Glue the overlapping edges of the paper together at the back.

3. Cut the two orange paper sheets down to 8 1/2" x 5". Use your scissors (zigzag, wavy, or deckle edged) to cut 1/2" strips vertically up to 1 1/2" from the top of the two sheets of orange paper.

4. Apply glue along the solid, uncut, top edge of the orange paper hair. Center and wrap the hair around the back side of the can. Placing uncut edge flush to top edge of the can, press in place.

5. Using a pencil (or straight-edged scissors), *carefully* curl each orange paper strip upward or under. Vary the tightness of the curl and curling direction with every other strip to give the hair a random, ragged, and straggled look.

6. Hat brim—Follow the instructions for Step 2 of Mr. Snowman on page 58.

7. Using the black marker, outline the white eye piece. Color in the dots for the pupils of the eyes. Apply a thin, smooth coat of glue to the back side. Carefully slide the eyes just under the hat rim, centered in the face area, and press in place.

8. Roll the green quarter circle piece to form a tight cone-shaped nose. The edges will overlap about 1/4". Glue the edges together. Allow the glue to set and dry. Crumple and crush the green cone-shaped nose to give it a crooked, old look. Fold and roll the wart piece into a little wad. Apply glue to the underside of the wart, and position it anywhere on the nose. Fold in about 1/2" edge of paper at the base of the nose cone. Apply hot glue to the folded base of the nose, and press it in place just under the eyes.

9. Apply a thin, smooth coat of glue to the back side of the black paper mouth piece. Center it near the bottom of the can, and glue it in place. Decide where you want the small, white tooth pieces, and glue them in place.

10. Roll the large, black quarter circle of butcher paper to form a cone. Using the top edge of the can as a guide, adjust the bottom opening of the cone so that it will fit nicely over the edge of the can and can be removed easily. Glue the overlapping edges.

11. Glue the purple ribbon around the hat, about 1" from the bottom. Center the yellow, square buckle in the front, and glue it on top of the purple ribbon. Glue the funky yellow die cut shapes on the hat.

12. Crush and crumple the top of the hat to give it the old witchy look.

13. Fill your Witchy Poo full of goodies, or set her out to scare away unwanted Halloween ghoulies.

This fun Halloween container is just another way to give goodies, trick-or-treat candies, or just use as a fun Halloween decoration. Be sure not to cross her path, or she might put a spell on you!

Morty the mummy

MATERIALS:

- 1 clean 7" x 4 1/4" diameter can (pineapple juice or tomato juice)
- 6 3/4" x 14" green paper
- 2 yards (approx.) of 2" wide strips of ripped muslin or your choice of material
- Scrap of black construction paper
- White card stock paper
- Fine point black marker
- Thick craft glue
- Eyes and mouth pattern (page 82)

INSTRUCTIONS

1. Trace and cut out the pattern pieces (inner eye—white; outer eye—purple; mouth—black).

2. Wrap the green paper piece around the can, and glue it in place.

3. Start to wrap the 2" ripped muslin randomly and unevenly around the can, all the way down to the bottom and back up toward the top again, until you come to the end of the strip. Glue the fabric in place, leaving 1" to 1 1/2" sticking out.

4. Tuck the black eye piece under a fabric strip, and glue it in place about a third of the way down from the top of the can.

5. Draw pupils on the white eye piece. Apply a thin, smooth coat of glue to the back side of the eyes, and carefully slide the eyes just under the strip of fabric and in front of the black eye shadow piece. Press in place.

6. Create an opening between the fabric strips to glue the black mouth piece.

7. You might want to dab glue on a few of the fabric strips to secure them in place.

Morty will give your Halloween treats a nice, wrapped-up feeling. Create him along with all of his other Halloween buddies to create a collection to scare away the heebie-jeebies or to just tickle your funny bone.

TEACHER PROJECT

tips — SUGGESTIONS

You could paint the eyes and teeth of the Halloween projects with Glow in the Dark paint, or cut them out of specialty Glow in the Dark paper or sticker film. For a neat effect, place all the projects with glow in the dark eyes and teeth sitting on a shelf or mantel peering at you through the dark. My children sure get a big kick out of them.

Mr. jack with black cat

When the pattern is photocopied at 63%, it then fits a 1 lb. pie filling, large pineapple, or small powdered hot cocoa can, which may be more accessible for the student to bring from home.

MATERIALS:

- 1 clean #10 can with lid
- 6 3/4" x 20" orange butcher paper or two sheets of 8 1/2" x 11" orange construction paper
- 1 sheet of 8 1/2" x 11" black butcher paper or construction paper
- 1 sheet of 8 1/2" x 11" green card stock or felt
- 7 1/2" x 18" green, stretchy, knit material
- White gel pen
- Green fine point marker
- Hot glue gun
- Paper glue stick
- Two green pipe cleaners (chenille stems) 12" x 15mm
- Green rubber band or a few strands of raffia
- A large handful of stuffing/batting or shredded tissue paper
- Mr. Jack with cat and leaf patterns (page 84)

INSTRUCTIONS

1. Measure, cut, and wrap the orange paper around the can. Glue it in place where the paper overlaps itself.

2. Trace and cut pattern pieces (Mr. Jack face, cat, and leaf pieces out of the black paper, and two leaves from the green paper).

HERE'S ANOTHER fun HALLOWEEN CONTAINER THAT'S EASY AND fAST TO MAKE.

3. Center and glue (paper glue) the black pieces to the front of can.

4. Using the white gel pen, draw the eyes and nose on the cat. With the green marker, draw the leaf lines on the green leaves.

5. Hot glue the side edges of the green knit material to create a tube. Stretch and slide the tube over the plastic lid, with 1" to 2" overhanging the underside of the lid. Glue the tube in place on the underside of lid.

6. Place the lid on top of the can, and place the desired amount of stuffing into the opening of the tube on top of the lid. Tie off with rubber band and raffia.

7. Center and glue one end of a green pipe cleaner to the back side of each of the green paper leaves. Wrap the pipe cleaner around the rubber band area of the hat. Coil the remaining pipe cleaner stems around a pen or pencil to create the look of coiling vines.

tips & SUGGESTIONS

Frankie and Mr. Jack with Black Cat containers could easily be made into Trick or Treat pails by punching or drilling holes on each side of the metal can and threading #20 gauge craft wire through to make a handle. Wrap and glue a 3" x 6" piece of black craft foam around the middle of the craft wire to make a hand cushion. Then you'll have a sturdy and decorative Trick or Treat pail.

young tom turkey

🍎 **TEACHER PROJECT** By photocopying the pattern to 75%, the project then fits the smaller recycled tomato sauce or mandarin orange cans, which may be more accessible for the student to bring from home.

MATERIALS:

- 1 clean 3 1/2" x 5 1/4" diameter can with lid (I used an Almond Roca Can)
- 3 sheets of 8 1/2" x 11" rusty brown card stock paper
- Half sheets of 8 1/2" x 11" bright yellow, white, red and green pieces of card stock or poster board
- Fine point black permanent marker
- Paper glue stick
- Thick craft glue
- Tom Turkey pattern (page 85)

TOM MAKES A NICE TABLE OR SHELF DECORATION AS AN EMPTY CAN, bUT AS A NEW CAN full of NUTS OR CANdy, COVERED WITH his bRIGHTly COlORED TAIL fEATHERS, HE'S JUST AS SMART AS A SPECIAl gIfT Of THANKSgIVINg.

INSTRUCTIONS

1. Measure, cut, cover, and glue brown card stock around the can.

2. Use the top half of the remaining sheet of brown card stock to cut a circle, 4 3/8" diameter. Use the bottom half for the turkey body pattern.

3. Trace the body pattern on the brown card stock, and cut it out. Trace the collar, feet, beak, and three different tail feathers onto colored papers, and cut them out.

4. Glue the colored pieces (feet, beak, white collar, and red beak over hang) onto Tom's body. Glue the tail feathers on top of each other.

5. Draw the pupils of the eyes and bow on the collar with permanent black marker.

6. Glue the back side of Tom's body to the front of the can. Center and glue the front of the yellow tail feathers to the back of the can and over the paper seam. (Be careful not to glue the pieces to the lip of the lid.) Glue the brown circle on top of the lid to cover any graphics or printing.

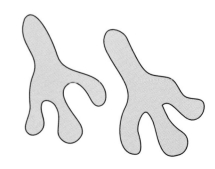

pilgrims & indians

TEACHER PROJECT Remember to spray paint enough pudding cups ahead of time, if you have male students who choose to create John Pilgrim. Another alternative is to have the students color the pudding cups with black marker or crayons. Though I think the marker technique could get a little messy, experiment and see what works best.

These are quick and easy. Save your cans and your pudding and condiment cups to create enough Pilgrim or Indian cups for each one of your Thanksgiving dinner guests. Place nicely written place cards in front of the cups. They will definitely become a special treat at the children's table.

MATERIALS:

- 4 clean 3" x 2 5/8" diameter cans (I used 8 oz. tomato sauce cans)
- 1 clean pudding cup container for John's hat
- 1 white, plastic condiment cup with 3" diameter at the top for Betsy's bonnet
- 1 small, red craft feather (or homemade paper feather) for Red Feather's headband
- 1 sheet of 8 1/2" x 11" white bond paper
- 1 sheet of 8 1/2" x 11" light brown bond paper or brown paper bag
- Black spray paint
- Crayons, color pencils, markers, or paint
- Craft glue and scissors
- Pilgrims and Indians patterns (page 86–87)

INSTRUCTIONS

1. Photocopy or trace the patterns onto the sheets of white and brown bond paper.

2. Following painting instruc- tions on page 8, paint the pudding cup container with black paint.

3. Color in the Pilgrims and Indians patterns. Remember to color the small square buckle for John Pilgrim. Cut the pattern pieces out along the solid line.

4. Center the individual patterns, and wrap them around a clean tomato sauce can. Glue them in place. Fold the overhanging paper, and glue it inside the cans. Glue the bottom excess to the bottom of the cans.

5. Turn the black, painted pudding cup upside down. Glue the buckle piece to the front side of the cup.

6. Snip the small lines on the brim of Betsy's white bonnet. Fold the tabs, and glue them along the edge, just inside the lip of the white condiment cup.

7. Glue a feather to the back of Red Feather's (Indian man) can. If you'd like, you could glue a small feather to the side and in front of Bubbling Brook's (Indian lady) can.

8. Fill the cans with nuts and small candy. Set them out along the table settings or on the shelf as decoration.

tips — SUGGESTIONS

Create these cups as a pre-dinner craft activity. Allow the children to craft their own cups. Make sure you have enough spray-painted, black cups prepared ahead of time.

angels

Special Tools Needed:

- 1" foam brush (I used Loew-Cornell 1")
- Small, flat-head screwdriver

Materials:

- 2 clean potato chip canisters with plastic lids, 3.5 oz. and 6 oz. sizes
- Gold and silver spray paint
- 2, 2 1/2" diameter foam balls (I used Kreative Foam by Design A Line Inc.)
- 3 sheets of 8 1/2" x 11" preprinted scrapbook paper or gift wrap paper, one of each color (I used white/cream, gold, and silver Diamond Dust paper card stock with coordinating Diamond Dust scattered star pattern papers by Paper Adventures)
- Gold, silver, white, and black 1/8" curling ribbon or gold and silver Christmas tree icicles
- 2 tinsel stem pipe cleaners 12" x 15mm (one gold, one silver)
- Hot glue and thick craft glue
- Extra fine point black permanent marker
- Pink gel pen
- Acrylic craft paints (I used Apple Barrel Colors by Plaid)
- Silver angel face, darker toned flesh color (I used #20558 Territorial Beige)
- Gold angel face, lighter toned flesh color (I used #20509 English Lace)
- Angel and angel wings patterns (pages 88–89)

These angels joyfully sing praises of Hallelujah. They make charming decorations for the mantel, but remember they can be gift containers filled with candy and treats to give away.

Instructions

1. Follow the general paint instructions on page 8 to spray paint the 6 oz. canister and lid gold. Paint the 3.5 oz. canister and lid silver.

2. Using a 1" brush, paint the foam balls—one in darker tone; one in lighter tone. Set them aside to dry.

3. Trace the star and inner wing patterns onto the back side of the Diamond Dust card stock—one silver, the other gold. Trace the horizontal outer wing and short gown pattern shapes onto white card stock. Trace the vertical outer wing and long gown onto the white/cream card stock. Cut all of the pieces out.

4. Cut a 5 1/4" x 10" piece from the silver star patterned paper.

Wrap and hot glue it around the silver-painted 3.5 oz. canister. Trim 1" from a sheet of 8 1/2" x 11" gold star patterned paper, and wrap the 8 1/2" x 10" piece around the gold-painted 6 oz. canister. Hot glue it in place.

5. Wrap and glue the short, white gown piece around the silver-painted 3.5 oz. canister. Wrap and glue the long, cream/white gown piece around the gold-painted 6 oz. canister.

6. Trace the face patterns onto the painted balls, and draw in the lip lines with the pink gel pen. Draw in the eye, nose, and open mouth lines with the extra fine point black marker.

7. Curly Angel Hair—Cut four 18" strands of curling ribbon from each of the silver, gold metallic, black, and white ribbon. Put the black and silver strands together in a bunch and the gold and white strands (I added thin gold icicles) in a bunch. Tie a knot in the middle of each of the bunches. Cut the ribbon strands vertically into thinner strands, and curl the strands to various lengths and tightnesses. Place the knotted section of the curly ribbon bunches at the center

top of the painted ball heads. Using a small, flat-head screwdriver, gently push and poke the curly ribbon hair 1/2" into the foam ball heads.

8. Cut a few strands of silver and gold ribbon. Cut the ribbon strands into thinner strands. Glue the strands to the back side of the stars, and glue the stars to the front of the canisters. Curl the ribbon strands.

9. Create halos from the silver and gold pipe cleaners. Glue the halos to the back side of the heads.

10. Glue the heads to the plastic lids. Glue the inner wing pieces to the outer wing pieces, and glue the wings to the back side of the canisters. Be sure not to glue the wings to the plastic lid edge, so the lid can be removed.

Nativity

Materials:

- 1 clean #10 can with white lid
- 1 Nativity die cut from Creative Memories Christmas Collection (cut off star on top of the stable)
- 2 sheets of 8 1/2" by 11" preprinted scrapbook paper (I used Item #42-5228 sheet of Night Sky by Jeff Goodsell, Provo Craft) or make your own starry sky background with dark paper and a white gel pen
- 1 white gift bow
- Paper glue
- 1 sheet of 8 1/2" by 11" white card stock paper for star highlights
- Nativity background star pattern (page 90)

Instructions

1. Wrap the dark sky paper around the can, and glue it in place where the paper overlaps itself.

2. Photocopy or trace the star pattern. Cut the star shapes out, and glue them in front of the background sky paper.

3. Glue the nativity die cut in front of the white star pattern.

4. Fill the can with goodies, place the bow on top, and give it away.

This Christmas can gives an ambiance of reverence, in remembrance of that night long ago when the Baby Jesus was born. Fill the can full of gifts homemade and from the heart, and it becomes an excellent way to say "Merry Christmas!"

tips & SUGGESTIONS

With all the wonderful die cuts available, you could create any Christmas design or pattern covering for a gift container. Go create and enjoy!

hanukkah

 TEACHER PROJECT You could photocopy the Hanukkah pattern and have the students paint, color, and wrap the design around the can. Write in Happy Hanukkah with a marker or crayon. The pattern can be reduced 63% to be wrapped around a smaller 1 lb. pie filling can.

MATERIALS:

- 1 clean #10 can
- 1 piece of 6 3/4" by 20" white gift wrap or white butcher paper
- Making Memories Little Letters Varsity Shadow Gold Item #16040
- 1/2 sheet of gold card stock
- 3" x 3" scrap of blue foil card stock or blue card stock
- 12 1/2" of 1/8" blue satin ribbon
- Fine tip yellow permanent marker
- 2 to 3 yards of 3/8" blue metallic gift wrapping ribbon
- 2 to 3 yards of 5/8" gold gift wrapping ribbon
- Hanukkah pattern (page 90)

INSTRUCTIONS

1. Wrap white paper around the can, and glue it in place.

2. Trace the Menorah candleholder and Hebrew language symbol pattern pieces onto the backside of the gold foil card stock. Trace the dreidel pattern shape to the back side of the blue card stock. Cut out the pattern pieces. Glue the gold Hebrew symbols to the front of the blue dreidel piece.

Hanukkah is a winter season holiday that is celebrated by the Jewish people. It commemorates their victory over the Syrians long ago. The candleholder is called a Menorah. The star of David is the symbol of Jewish heritage. The dreidel is a top-like toy that the children play with. Create this symbolic Hanukkah can, and fill it with gifts.

3. Glue the gold Menorah and blue dreidel to the front of the can.

4. Trace the star of David onto the front of the can. Cut the blue satin ribbon in half, and glue the pieces in the outline of the triangles that make the star of David.

5. Cut nine 1/4" x 5/8" pieces from the blue metallic ribbon, and glue each one of these as candles above the menorah candleholder. Draw candle flames above the blue candles with the yellow marker.

6. Use the gold stickers to spell out Happy Hanukkah.

7. Cut and wrap 20" lengths of gold ribbon around the top and bottom areas of the can. Place 20" lengths of blue ribbon on top of the gold ribbons. With the leftover ribbon, cut strips of varied widths, and curl them (carefully, with a straight-edge scissors) to create a decorative bow. Place the bow on top.

8. Fill the can with traditional foods or gifts.

tips SUGGESTIONS

Substitute silver ribbon, card stock, and silver letter stickers in place of the gold.

Snowflake pictures

Special tool option:

- Circle cutter or circle ruler

Materials:

- 1 clean #10 can with white lid
- 2 sheets of 8 1/2" x 11" pre-printed snowflake scrapbook paper or decorative gift wrap (I used two 8 1/2" x 11" sheets of item #42-6255 Snowflurries by Kristin Cook, Provo Craft)
- Many snowflake die cuts in white card stock paper (I used Ellison die cuts)
- Photos of children
- 1/2 sheet of 8 1/2" x 11" white card stock

Instructions

1. Trim scrapbook paper or gift wrap to 6 3/4" x 11". Wrap the paper around the can, and glue it in place.

2. Using a circle cutter or template, cut the children's faces from the photos so they will fit nicely in the center of the snowflakes. Cut circle frames from white card stock. Center and glue the photo circles on top of the snowflake die cuts. Glue the circle frames over the photos. Glue the snowflakes on the front and all around the can.

3. Have the kids help make cookies, candy, and goodies to fill up the can. Place a pretty gift bow on top. What grandmother wouldn't be just tickled to receive a gift like this?

This is a great gift container to give to grandparents and relatives with pictures of the children. Real snowflakes are unique and different from each other, so how appropriate to use them to frame each individual child's picture. It's possible to place up to ten snowflake frames on one #10 can.

tips — SUGGESTIONS

Consider flower die cuts, framing children's pictures, and coordinating decorative background as a nice Mother's Day gift. Or, try sport ball die cuts framing pictures for Father's Day.

Kwanzaa

 **TEACHER PROJECT** You could photo-copy the Kwan-zaa pattern and have the students paint, color, and wrap the design around the can.

Special tools:

- #4 shader paint brush (I used Loew-Cornell #4 shader Comfort 3300)

Materials:

- 1 clean #10 can with optional lid
- 6 3/4" x 20" background paper (I used two 8 1/2" x 11" sheets of light brown parchment-col-ored card stock.)
- Acrylic paints or opaque paint markers; test on card stock to see color application (I used Delta Ceramcoat acrylic paints.)
- Light green—Apple Green #02076
- Green—Kelly Green #02052
- Red—Crimson #02076
- Yellow—Opaque yellow #02509
- Fine point permanent black marker
- Kwanzaa pattern (page 91)

INSTRUCTIONS

1. Photocopy or trace the Kwanzaa pattern onto a sheet of 8 1/2" x 11" background paper. Trim the paper to 6 3/4" x 10 1/2". Trim the other paper to 6 3/4" x 9 1/2". Glue the papers together to create one continuous length of paper, 6 3/4" x 20". Trace the bot-tom Kwanzaa border onto the other sheet of paper, 5 1/4" up from the bottom, to create a con-tinuous border.

Kwanzaa is a cultural celebration that highlights and honors the values and principles of the African people. The holiday begins on December 26 and goes to January 1.
The symbolic colors of Kwanzaa are also the colors of the flag (Bendera). Black is for the color of the people; red is for the blood shed in the fight for freedom; and green is for the fertile crops of the homeland and the work of the people.

2. First, paint in the pattern with red, green, and yellow. Allow it to dry. Outline the colored areas and fill in the black areas with black marker.

3. Wrap the background paper around the can, and glue it in place.

4. Fill the can with traditional foods or gifts—fruits, nuts, vegeta-bles, or creative handmade gifts. Harambee! (Let us all work together!) Enjoy!

Christmas birdhouse garland

Special Tools Needed:

- Decorative cutting edge scissors (I used Fiskars Paper Edgers, Regular, Seagull)
- Large-eye darning needle
- Craft knife

Materials:

- 6–12, 3 oz. Dixie bathroom cups in the bluebirds design
- Fine point permanent red, green, and black markers
- 5 yards of 1/8" white or red satin ribbon or 1mm satin cord
- 2 sheets of 8 1/2" x 11" red card stock
- Hot glue
- Finely-shredded tissue paper, straw-colored raffia, or excelsior

Instructions

1. Color over all the blue on the birds with red markers to make red Christmas birds. Make small, red circles and dots over the pink flowers to transform them into red Christmas berries.

2. Color over the leaves with the green marker. Use straight angled lines in the direction of the leaf growth to resemble evergreen needles. If you'd like, color over and redefine the little black eyes and beaks.

3. Mark a 3 3/4" diameter circle roof from the red card stock for each birdhouse cup. Cut circles out with decorative edge scissors (remember to go slowly and realign the cutting edge when using decorative edged scissors to

achieve a continued, even-patterned edge).

4. Following the instructions for the beverage birdhouse roofs, step 6 on page 37, assemble the roofs, and glue them to the top rims of cups.

5. Optional — Mark and cut (with a craft knife) 1/2" diameter circle holes in the front of each cup and tuck a small amount of shredded tissue into the holes, giving the impression of nesting material.

6. Thread the darning needle with your choice of ribbon or cording. Poke through 3/8" down from the tip of the conical roofs, and thread the birdhouses onto the ribbon. Space the birdhouses along the ribbon.

7. String garland on the tree or over the mantel.

This craft project could become a fun family activity. Get the whole family involved in re-coloring these cups and cutting out the roofs. Several hands make quick work of a lengthy garland. The project instructions given are for five yards. If more is needed for a larger tree, just double or triple the cups, red paper, and ribbon amounts.

tips — SUGGESTIONS

For springtime, eliminate re-coloring the cups, and apply blue roofs. Use the garland as a decoration on a silk house tree or hanging across the front porch.

rodney reindeer

TEACHER PROJECT

MATERIALS:

- 1 clean 1 lb. can (pumpkin or pie filling)
- 4 3/8" x 13" cut from a brown paper bag or brown craft paper
- 1 sheet of 8 1/2" x 11" brown chip board (very lightweight cardboard) or light brown poster board
- 3" x 3" or larger scraps of colored construction or card stock paper in yellow, beige, and red
- Fine point black permanent marker
- Thick craft glue and paper glue stick
- Rodney the Reindeer pattern (page 93)

INSTRUCTIONS

1. Wrap and glue the brown paper around the can.

2. Trace Rodney onto the brown chip board/poster board, and cut him out. Lightly trace the facial features as a guide for the eyes and mouth. Trace the star, hair, and nose onto scrap pieces of colored paper, and cut them out.

3. Glue the hair, nose, and star pieces onto Rodney's face and antler.

4. Use your permanent black marker to draw the pupils of the eyes and the detail lines for the mouth and ears.

5. Glue the back side of Rodney's face to the can, covering the paper seam. Fill Rodney with goodies.

Rodney is another super easy and quick project to make. He makes a really nice, small gift container. Put something tasty inside, and give him to a co-worker.

tips & SUGGESTIONS

Rodney Reindeer, Santa, Mr. Snowman, and Perry Penguin can be filled with Kettle style popcorn, brownies, holiday cookies, and candies. They fast became a sure fire hit when presented as a neighbor gift and at elderly care homes throughout the festive holiday season.

Santa

MATERIALS:

- 1 clean #10 can with lid
- 6 3/4" x 20" white gift wrap or butcher paper
- 1/2 sheet of 8 1/2" by 11" pink card stock paper for body pattern
- 7 1/2" x 18" red, stretchy knit material
- Heavy white felt sheet or white paper card stock:
  - 20 3/4" x 1 1/4" for wavy hatband
  - 3/4" x 4" for hat ring band
  - Scrap pieces for eyebrows, mustache, and beard shapes
- Large handful stuffing/batting or shredded tissue paper
- One 1 1/2" or 2" diameter white pom pom
- Red and blue permanent markers
- Hot glue or craft glue
- Paper glue stick
- Rubber band
- Pink chalk
- Santa pattern (page 92)

This jolly fellow expresses a definite "Happy Holidays" to all who receive him. He makes a great gift container to give to neighbors and coworkers.

INSTRUCTIONS

1. Wrap white paper around the can, and glue it in place.

2. Trace the face pattern onto the pink card stock, and cut it out. Trace over the mouth, nose, and eye lines with the red and blue markers. Lightly blush cheeks with pink chalk.

3. Trace and cut out the eyebrows, mustache, and beard shapes from white felt or card stock.

4. Trace the wavy hatband line along the full length of the 20 3/4" white felt or card stock.

5. Center and glue (paper glue) the pink face circular shape to the front of the can. Position and glue the eyebrows and beard shapes.

Glue the mustache over the edges of the beard shapes.

6. Hot glue the side edges of the red knit material together to create a tube. Stretch and slide the tube over the plastic lid, leaving 1" to 2" overhanging the underside of the lid. Glue the edges to the underside of the lid. Place the lid on top of the can, and place the desired amount of stuffing into the opening of the tube. Tie off the tube with a rubber band. Wrap the white felt hat ring band around the lid, covering the rubber band. Glue it in place. Glue the white pom pom on the end.

7. Finish off by wrapping and gluing the wavy hatband around the red, covered lid edge.

8. In the jolly spirit of the Santa, fill up the can with goodies and give away.

tips — SUGGESTIONS

You could make this Santa without a hat; just use a large piece of red cellophane or tissue paper tucked inside the can. Fill inside the cellophane or tissue paper with goodies, gather the ends of the tissue at the top, and tie off with a ball of white curling ribbon. Glue the wavy white hatband around the top edge the can.

Mr. snowman

MATERIALS:

- 1 clean #10 can
- Small holly berry trim, Christmas decoration pick, or homemade cutouts
- 6 3/4" x 20" white butcher paper or gift wrap, or two sheets of 8 1/2" x 11" white card stock
- 2" x 20" black construction or butcher paper
- Black poster board for 9" diameter hat brim
- 1" x 20" red ribbon
- Black permanent marker
- Hot glue gun and glue
- Paper glue stick
- A scrap of orange construction paper or card stock for the carrot nose pattern (page 96)

INSTRUCTIONS

1. Photocopy or trace the snowman face pattern onto a sheet of white butcher paper. Mark the eye dots and mouth line with a black marker. Wrap paper around the can, and glue it in place where it overlaps.

2. Hat Brim

a. Cut a 9" diameter circle from the black poster board. Mark a 6" diameter circle in the center of the 9" circle. Inside the 6" circle, mark and cut out an inner center circle of 4" diameter. Clip 1" tabs from the center of the circle to the 6" marked diameter line.

b. Fold each of the tabs back toward the outer ring of the hat rim. Very gently slide the circle opening over the top of the can, until the circle rim is just far enough down that the top edges of

This super simple snowman will fill his part when you stuff him full of goodies and give him away, guaranteed to warm someone's heart.

the tabs line up with top edge of the can. Apply a dot of glue to the back side of each of the tabs, and press the tabs to the can to hold the hat brim in place.

c. Run a line of glue around the outside of the tabs, just above the crease of where the tabs and the rim of the hat meet. Place the 2" by 20" black construction or butcher paper strip over the tabs, with the bottom edge of the strip flush with the crease of the tabs and hat rim. Overlap the edges of the black paper strip above the area where the white paper overlapped at the back of the can (so the overlapping seams match up).

d. Run a line of glue along the top inside edge of the can, and fold the excess black paper inside of the can. Press in place. This gives a nice finished look to the top of the hat rim.

3. Center the red ribbon around the black hat area, and glue it in place. *Optional: Give Mr. Snowman a knit ski hat! See Perry Penguin #5 on the following page.*

4. Trace the carrot nose piece onto the orange construction paper. Cut it out, and glue it in place.

5. Glue the holiday decoration/pick in front of the hat. Fill the can with goodies, and give it away.

perry penguin

MATERIALS:

- 1 clean #10 can with lid
- 6 3/4" x 20" black butcher paper, or two sheets of 8 1/2" x 11" black construction paper
- 1/2 sheet of 8 1/2" x 11" white card stock paper for the body pattern
- 7 1/2" x 18" long, red, stretchy knit material
- Small holly berry trim, Christmas decoration pick, or homemade cutouts
- Black permanent marker
- Hot glue gun
- Paper glue stick
- Rubber band and a few strands of raffia
- 1 large handful stuffing/batting or shredded tissue paper
- Scraps of orange- or tangerine- colored card stock for the beak and feet pattern
- Perry the Penguin pattern (page 96)

INSTRUCTIONS

1. Wrap the black paper around the can, and glue in place where the paper overlaps itself.

2. Trace the pattern pieces onto selected papers (body–white; beak–orange; two feet–orange), and cut them out.

3. Center and glue (paper glue) the white body shape onto the front of the can. Position and glue the beak and feet onto the white body.

4. Use your black marker to draw the eyes.

5. Glue (hot glue) the side edges of the red knit material together to create a tube. Stretch and slide the tube over the plastic lid, with 1" to 2" overhanging the underside of the lid, and glue in place. Place the lid on top of the can, and stuff the tube with the stuffing/batting. Tie off the tube with a rubber band and raffia.

Perry will charm even the grumpiest of Holiday Humbugs. Pack him full of flavored popcorn or any tasty goodie, and he'll be one of the most remembered gifts of the season.

6. Finish by positioning and gluing (hot glue) the small holiday decoration on the knit hat.

Mr. cool candy container

MATERIALS:

- 1 clean, dark blue liquid detergent cap (I used mine off a Tide 50 fl. oz. bottle.)
- 1 clean, 5" x 3 1/2" diameter, white plastic Kool-Aid container
- 1 clean .6 oz. mushroom can, 2 3/4" x 2 1/2" diameter
- 2 3/4" x 9" white Bristol/card stock paper
- 7 1/2" x 1/2" red ribbon or colored paper strip
- 15" x 1" scrap material, colored felt, or ribbon (for scarf) (I used a scrap of red plaid material.)
- 2 strips of 2" x 1/8" red ribbon
- 3 buttons, round sticker dots, or colored punch paper circles
- 2 red 1" pom poms
- 1 white pipe cleaner 12" x 15mm
- Orange and black markers
- Extra strength plastic glue and hot glue
- Scrap of red felt or card stock
- Face and mitten patterns (page 77)

INSTRUCTIONS

1. Trace the face pattern onto the center of the white paper. Color the nose, eyes, and mouth with orange and black markers. Wrap and glue the face paper around the mushroom can. Be sure the can is right side up when you glue the face paper onto the can. This way the cap (hat) will settle into the can, and it can be glued to the inside rim.

2. Take the two red 2" x 1/8" ribbons. Glue 1/4" of each to the inside top of the mushroom can, one on each side. Attach the other end of the ribbons to the outside of the can, and spot glue them in place. Glue a red pom pom at the end of each ribbon. These will serve as earmuffs for your snowman.

3. Glue the 7 1/2" of 1/2" wide red ribbon around the detergent cap. Apply extra strength glue to the underside of the flanged edge of detergent cap, and place the cap on top of the face can.

4. Trace the mitten patterns, 4 times, on scrap red felt or paper, and cut them out. Glue two mittens together over each end of the pipe cleaner. Center the pipe cleaner horizontally across the top of the Kool-Aid lid, and hot glue it in place.

5. Using the extra strength glue, glue the bottom rim of the face can to the top center of the Kool-Aid lid—sandwiching the pipe cleaner arms between.

6. Set the project aside, and allow the glue to set and dry.

7. With the lid securely screwed on, glue the three buttons or place the paper circles down the front of the container.

8. Wrap and tie 15" of the 1" wide scrap material around the neck area of the face can to resemble a scarf. Pull horizontal threads

This candy container is sure to be well received anytime through the Winter season.

out of the ends to create a fringed look, or snip small segments on felt or ribbon. Spot glue the underside of scarf to hold it in place.

9. Unscrew Mr. Cool's upper body and fill him with your favorite bite-size candies. How "Cool" is that? When he is presented as a gift, the receiver will be thinking how "Cool" you are, for your kindness.

beverage cup trees

MATERIALS:

- Dark green spray paint
- Textured snow paint for the snowcapped trees (I used Snow-Tex by DecoArt)
- Confetti stickers for Christmas tree (I used Creative Memories)
- Multicolored mini star stickers and red Christmas ribbons for Christmas tree (I used Mrs. Grossman's)
- Bright yellow card stock with two stars cut out (see star pattern on Rodney Reindeer, page 93)

For small tree:
- 3 1/2" h. x 2 1/2" d. paper cone
- 3 3/8" h. x 2 1/2" d. kid cup
- 4 1/2" h. x 3" d. small cup

For medium tree:
- 3 1/2" h. x 2 1/2" d. paper cone cup
- 2 3/4" h. x 2 1/2" d. kid cup
- 4 1/2" h. x 3" d. small cup
- 5" h. x 3 1/2" d. medium cup

For tallest tree — (same as decorated Christmas tree):
- 3 1/2" h. x 2 1/2" d. paper cone
- 3 3/8" h. x 2 1/2" d. kid cup
- 4 1/2" h. x 3" d. small cup
- 5" h. x 3 1/2" d. medium cup
- 6 1/4" h. x 3 1/2" d. large cup

INSTRUCTIONS

1. From the top, open rim of each cup, cut 1/2" to 3/4" tabs, 1/3 way down, all the way around each of the cups to create fringed look. Gently curl each fringe around a pencil, in an outward direction.

2. See general & basic instructions on using spray paint, page 8. Paint all the cups with 3 to 4 even applications of spray paint on the outside and inside. Allow each coat to dry thoroughly.

3. Stack and glue the cups on top of each other, working with the largest to the smallest, and finishing with the cone cup on the very top.

4. Randomly apply stickers to the Christmas tree. On the other trees, paint snow on the edges and tips of the curled fringes to give a snow-capped look.

5. For the Christmas tree, glue the base of one of the stars at the top tip of the tree. Glue the other star onto the back side of that star.

THESE TREES MAKE QUICK, WHIMSICAL DECORATIONS TO SET ON THE SHELF OR MANTEL. OBSERVANT GUESTS WILL BE AMUSED AT THE FACT THAT THEY ARE MADE OUT OF YOUR BEVERAGE CUPS FROM YOUR LAST FAST FOOD DINNER RUN.

tips — SUGGESTIONS

You could decorate the trees with glitter, sequins, miniature Christmas ornaments, and 1/8" ribbon or cording. Another decorating suggestion would be to spray paint the cups white. After you assemble the cups together into trees, spray them with adhesive and sprinkle silver or gold glitter all over.

Key to my heart angel bear

MATERIALS:

- 1 clean #10 can
- 6 3/4" x 20" white butcher's paper, white gift wrap, or silver gift wrap
- 1/2 sheet of white poster board
- 1 sheet of 8 1/2" x 11" silver metallic foil card stock
- 1/2 sheet of 8 1/2" x 11" red metallic foil card stock
- Fine point permanent blue, red, and black markers
- Paper glue and craft glue
- Craft/utility knife
- Bear patterns (pages 94–95)

INSTRUCTIONS

1. Wrap, cover, and glue your paper in place around the can.

2. Lightly trace the bear and wings pattern onto white poster board. Trace the inner wings, ear holes, nose, and feet pad shapes onto the back side of the silver foil card stock. Trace a full heart with keyhole pattern onto the back side of your red foil card stock. Cut out the pattern shapes.

3. With paper glue, glue the silver foil pieces in place. Use your traced outlines as a guide.

4. Using the craft knife, cut the keyhole shape from the red foil heart, and cut along the curved outline of the paw hand lines. Slide the red foil heart, from the top, underneath the cut flaps of the paws.

This angel bear brings the sweetness of love to Valentine's Day. Fill him full of someone special's favorite sweets, and then brace yourself for the smiles, hugs, and kisses to come.

5. With the permanent markers, go over and outline the traced detail lines on the bear—blue eyes, red mouth, black thumbs and feet.

6. Cut the wings in half, and position them behind the bear's shoulders. Glue in place.

7. Glue the back side of the bear to the paper seam on the can. Tuck decorative tissue paper inside the can, and fill with Valentine sweets.

puffy pom pom hearts

MATERIALS:

- 1 clean #10 can (white lid optional)
- 6 3/4" x 20" white butcher or gift wrap
- 1/2 sheet of 8 1/2" x 11" red card stock
- Below is an approximate pom pom count. You may use more or less, depending how closely the pom poms are placed next to each other:
- 30+, 5mm white pom poms
- 125, 10mm white pom poms
- 26, 10mm red pom poms
- 42, 5mm red pom poms
- 80, 1/2" red pom poms
- 3, 12" bamboo shish-ka-bob skewers
- Red permanent marker or paint
- Craft glue
- Cupid die cut from red card stock paper (I used an Ellison die cut)
- Hearts pattern (page 78)

INSTRUCTIONS

1. Trace the hearts pattern so the pattern repeats across the length of the 6 3/4" x 20" white paper. There will only be enough room for two large hearts and two smaller hearts. There will be about a 3 1/2" blank space at the back where the paper will come together. I traced the smallest heart shape pattern to be centered in this blank space.

2. Wrap the paper around the can, and glue it in place where it overlaps itself.

3. Glue the red 10mm pom poms along the heart outlines.

4. Glue about forty red 1/2" pom poms in a row along each of the top and bottom edges.

This container makes a cheery statement of "Happy Valentine's Day" when you place a plant or floral bouquet inside and give it to your special Valentine. You could decorate a white plastic lid with a row of red pom poms, and cut a slit in the top. This makes a great Valentine mail collection can for cards received at school or the work place.

5. Fill in the red pom pom heart patterns with the white 10mm pom poms.

6. In a random and spread out manner, glue the 5mm red pom poms all over the outside of the can.

7. Color the 12" bamboo skewers with the red permanent marker or paint.

8. Trace and cut the small hearts out of red card stock, for the decoration picks.

9. Glue the white 5mm pom poms around the edge of the small red paper heart and on the bare bottom of the cupid die cut. Use the 10mm white pom poms around the edge of the other red paper heart.

10. Glue the back sides of the pom pom decorated paper shapes to the tops of bamboo skewers.

11. Place a floral bouquet in the container and accent with cupid and hearts picks.

PATTERNS

bathroom essentials holders

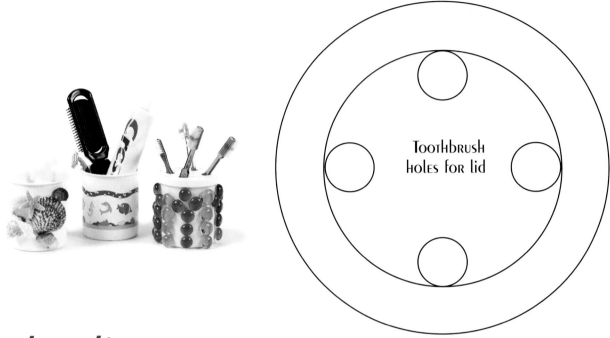

Toothbrush holes for lid

kokopeli can

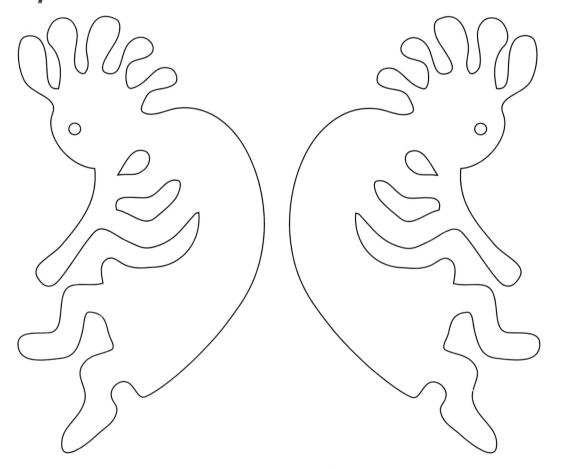

faux watering can

Flourish pattern (modified from Corel Print House clipart)

groovy wire candleholder

Wire guide
(Not shown at actual size.)

lighthouse trio

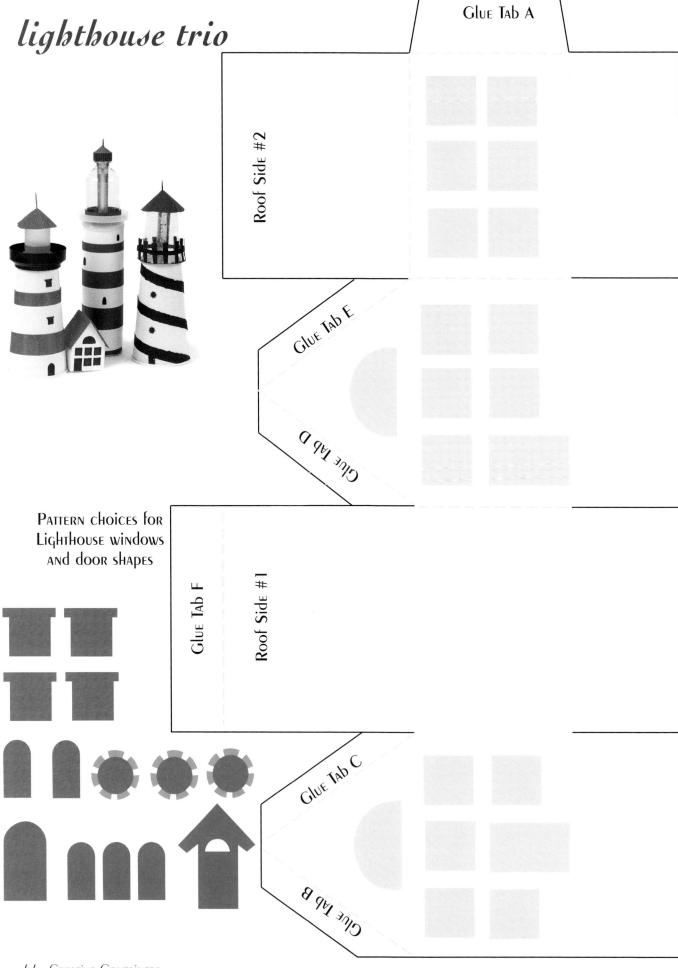

Glue Tab A

Roof Side #2

Glue Tab E

Glue Tab D

Glue Tab F

Roof Side #1

Pattern choices for Lighthouse windows and door shapes

Glue Tab C

Glue Tab B

Lighthouse roof and railing

Black lighthouse railing pattern

Diagram for positioning the blue lighthouse roof pattern on the plastic cap.

paper roof

plastic cap

Red and black lighthouse roof pattern
For the red lighthouse roof, DON'T fold along the dotted lines.

Blue lighthouse roof pattern for plastic cap

coin sorter bank

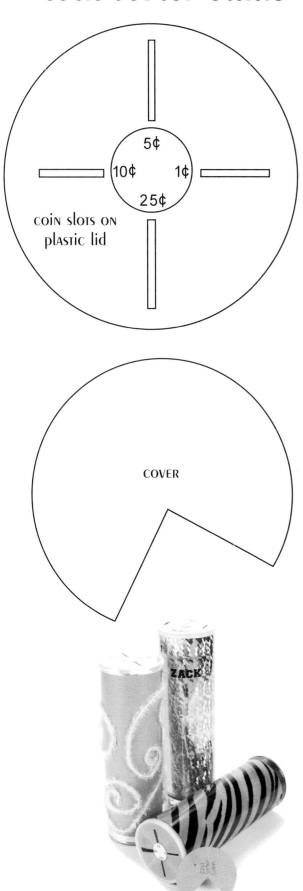

coin slots on plastic lid

5¢

10¢   1¢

25¢

COVER

2 13/16" wide

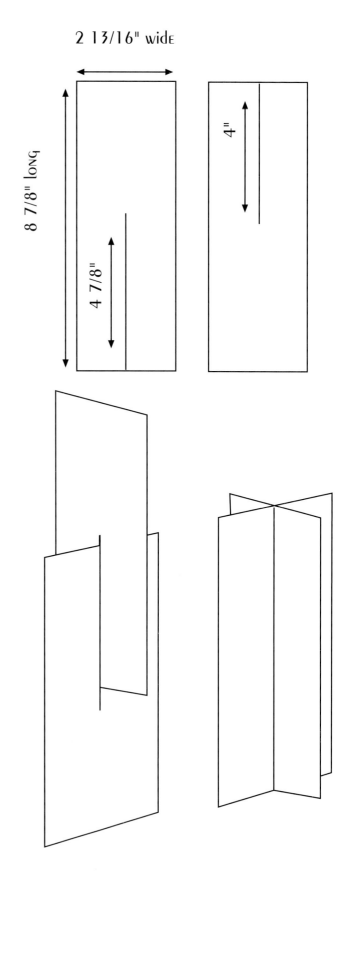

8 7/8" long

4 7/8"

4"

Circle hat rim
Kelly green

larry the leprechaun

Buckle—
bright
yellow

Face—pink
Eyebrows—orange

Bow tie—Kelly green
Clover leaf—light green

boris the bunny

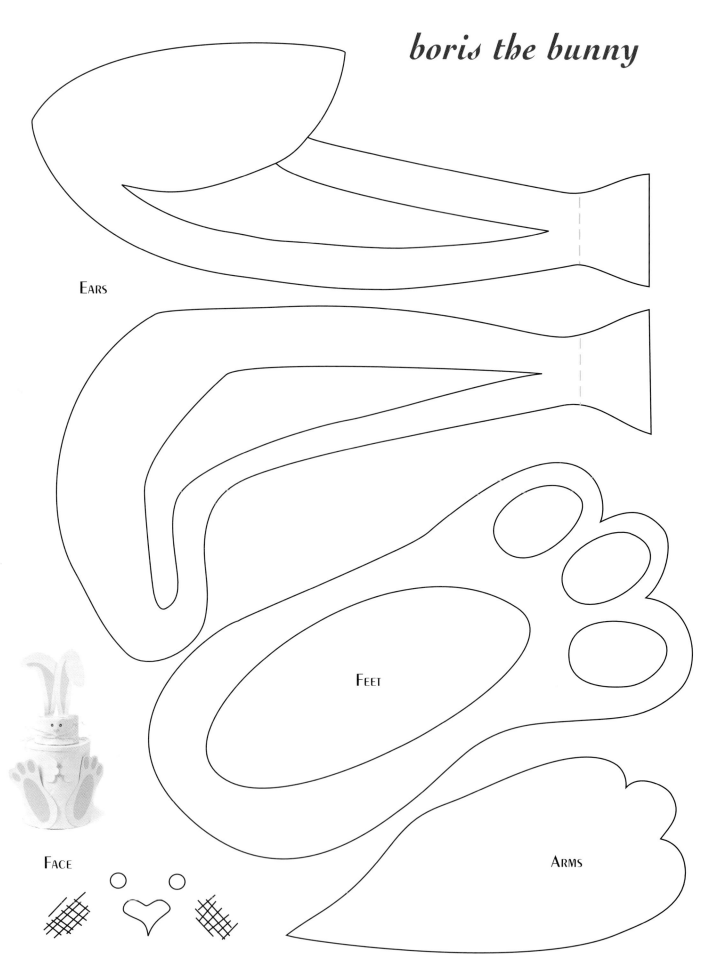

EARS

FEET

FACE

ARMS

faux watering can

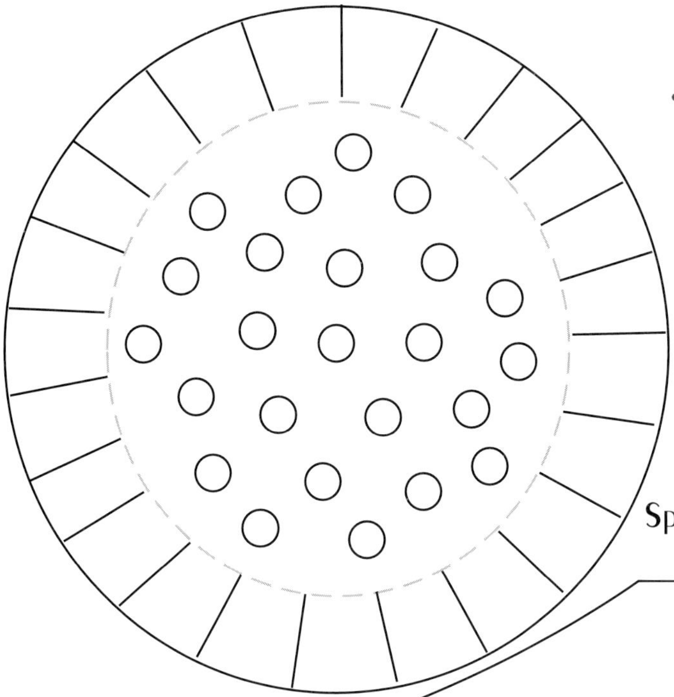

How to cut the Styrofoam brand foam core

1. Cut the top tip straight across.

2. Cut off the bottom at an angle.

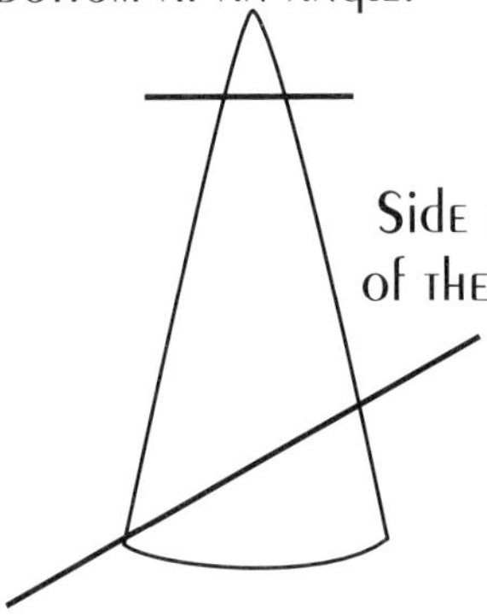

Side view of the cuts

3. Use a slow carving motion to achieve the best contour to fit the Styrofoam to the side of the can.

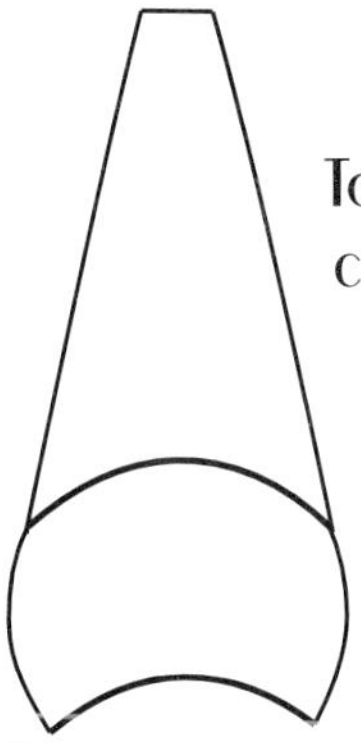

Top view of curved cut

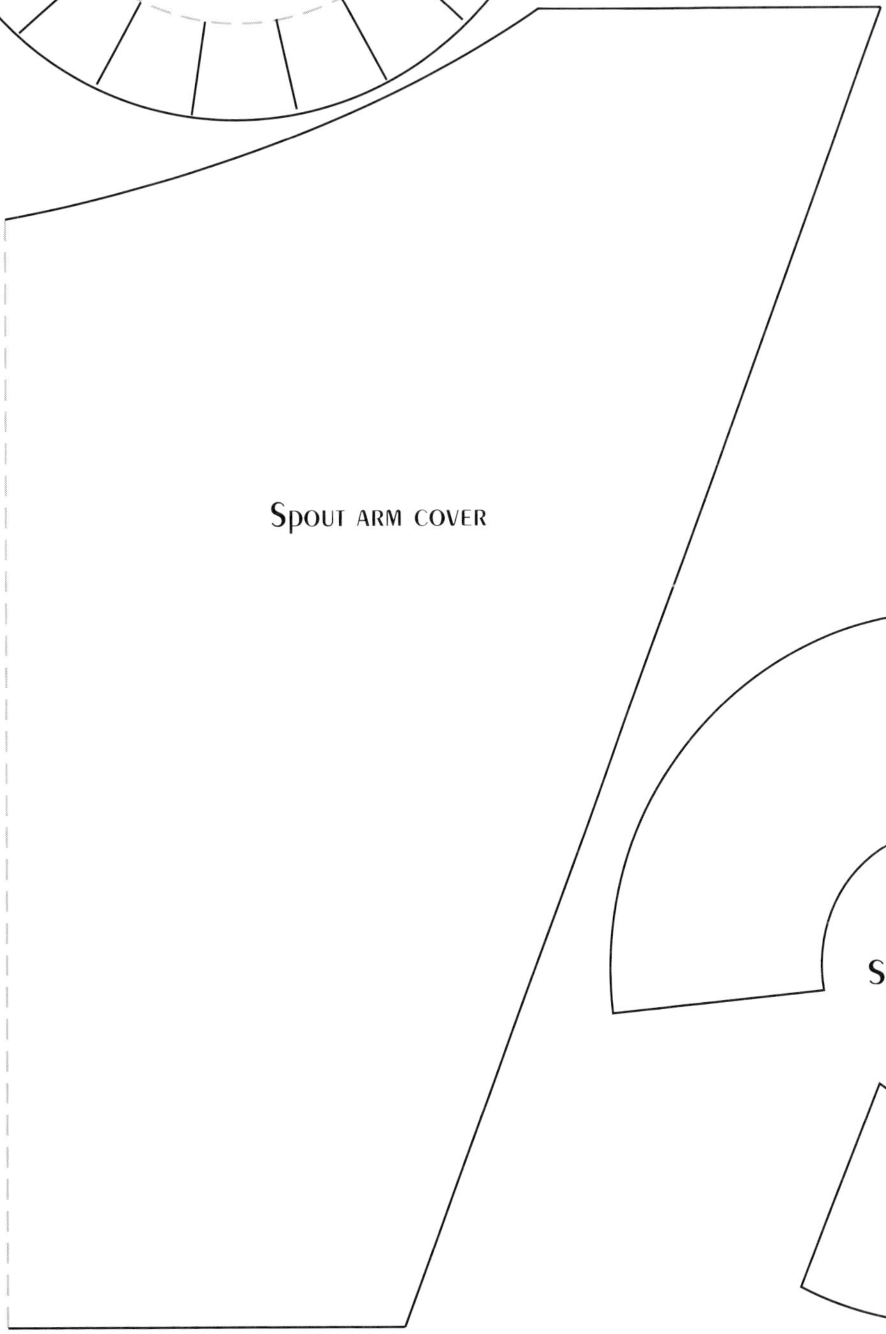

Sprinkle cap

Spout arm cover

Place on fold to create full size pattern

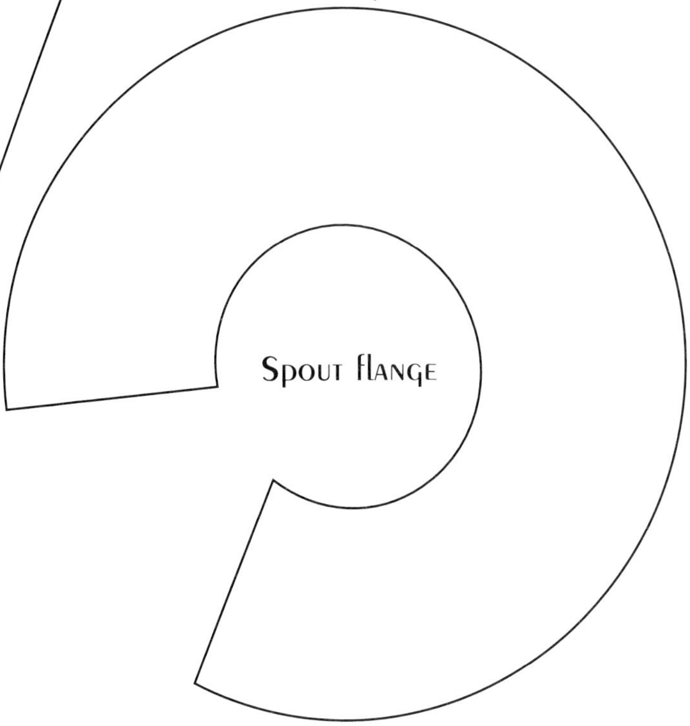

Spout flange

mini watering cans

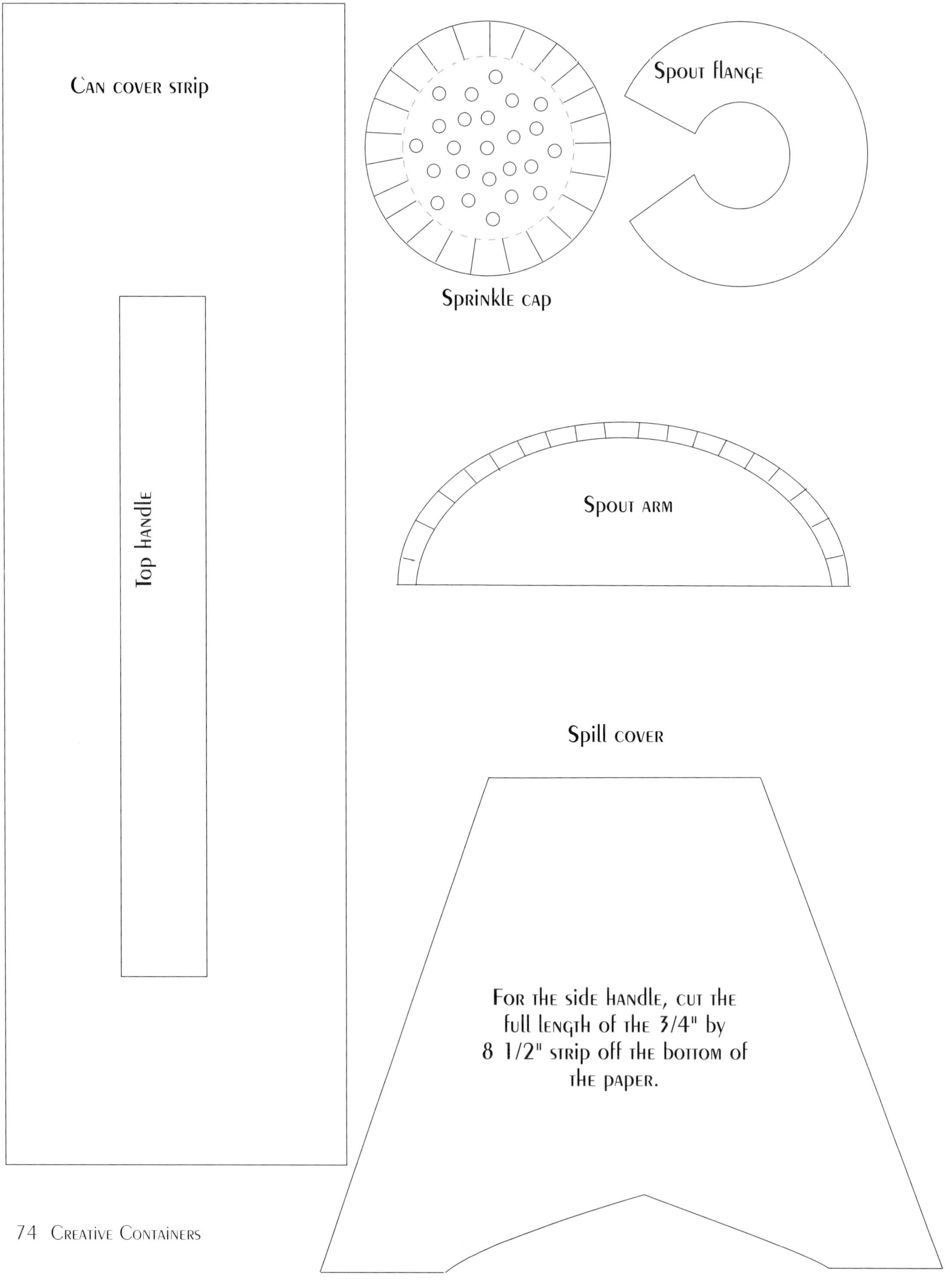

Can cover strip

Sprinkle cap

Spout flange

Top Handle

Spout arm

Spill cover

For the side handle, cut the full length of the 3/4" by 8 1/2" strip off the bottom of the paper.

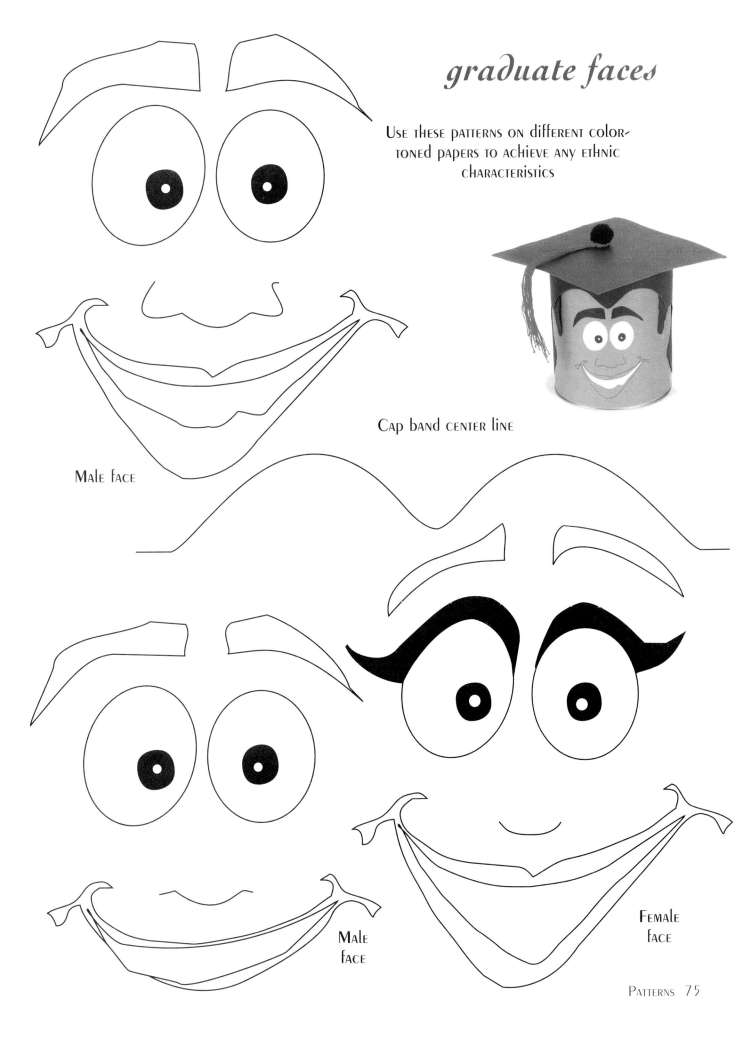

graduate faces

Use these patterns on different color-toned papers to achieve any ethnic characteristics

Cap band center line

Male face

Male face

Female face

American flag

dragonfly

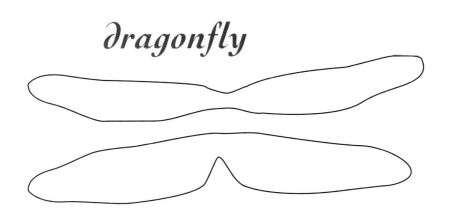

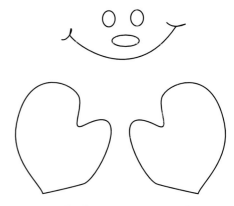

*birthday and
nursery clown*

mr. cool

*bridal shower
wedding cake*

TOPPER

freedom rockets

cap tops

pattern for 3 1/2" diameter cup top

These patterns could also be used for the beverage cup birdhouse roofs.

Rocket Cap pattern for toilet paper tubes.

puffy pom pom hearts

Trace the hearts in a row to repeat the pattern around the can.

count fangs

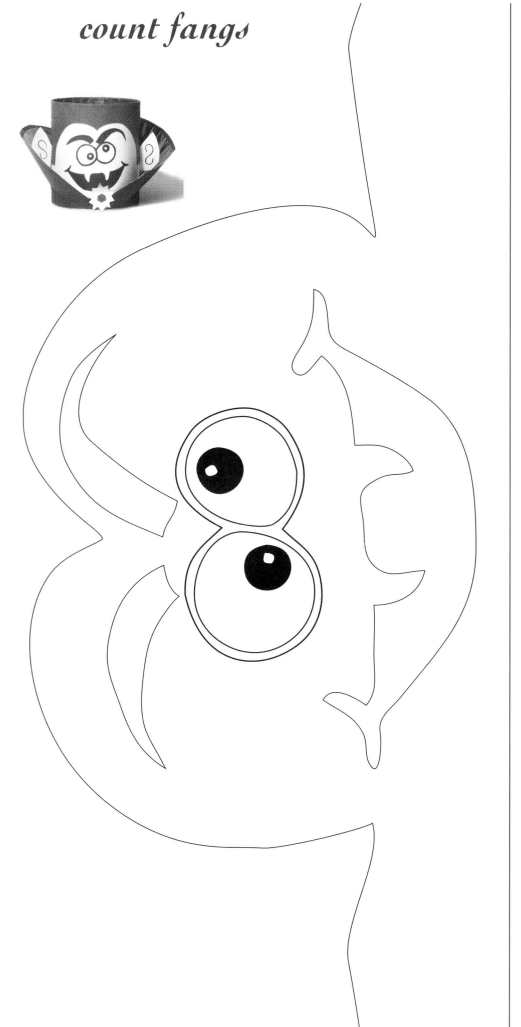

count fangs

Cape pattern

Place on fold

Ears

Fold in

Fold in

Place on fold

Main cape collar

Top cape piece
Tape across top of main cape piece to
create full cape pattern.

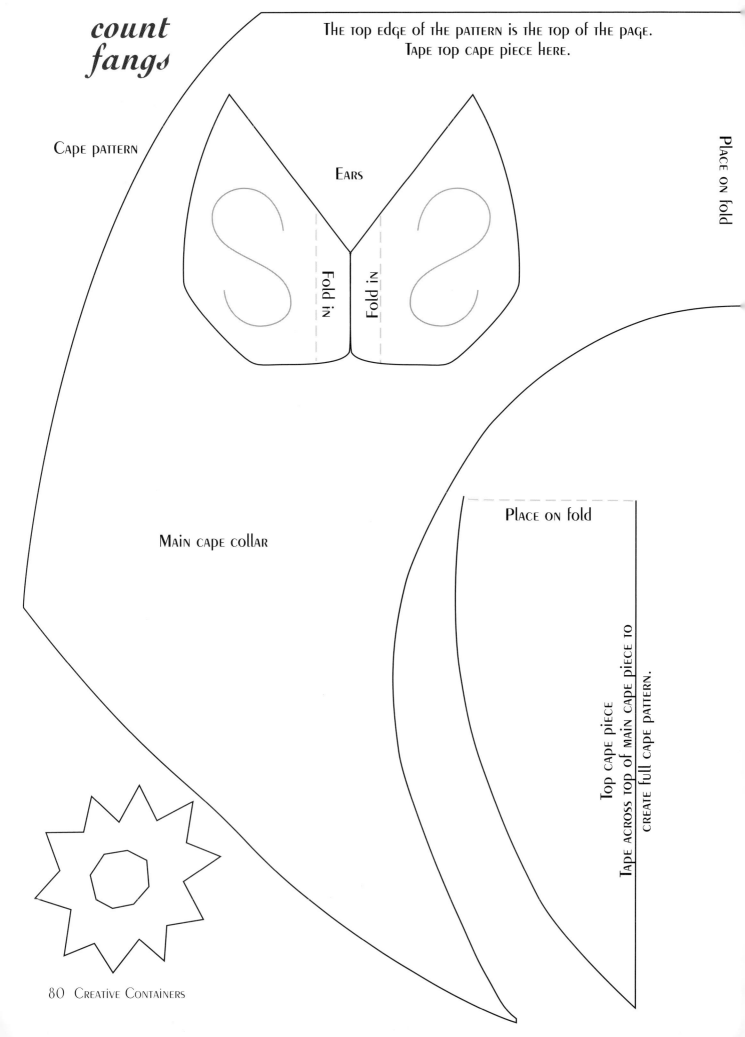

frankie

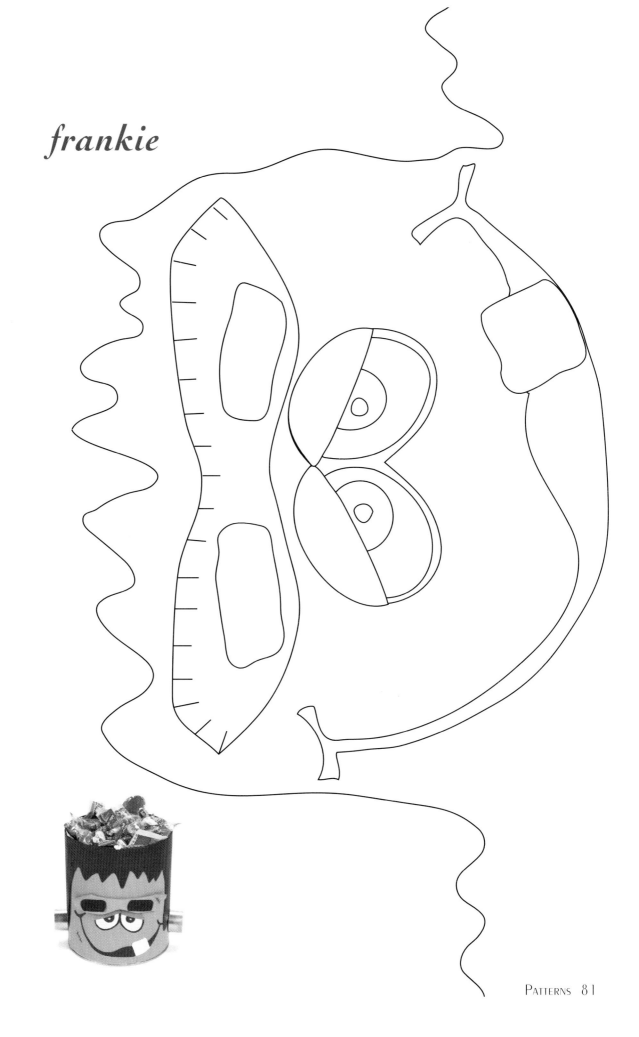

mr. batty

Morty the Mummy
Inner eye—white
Outer eye—black
Mouth shape—black

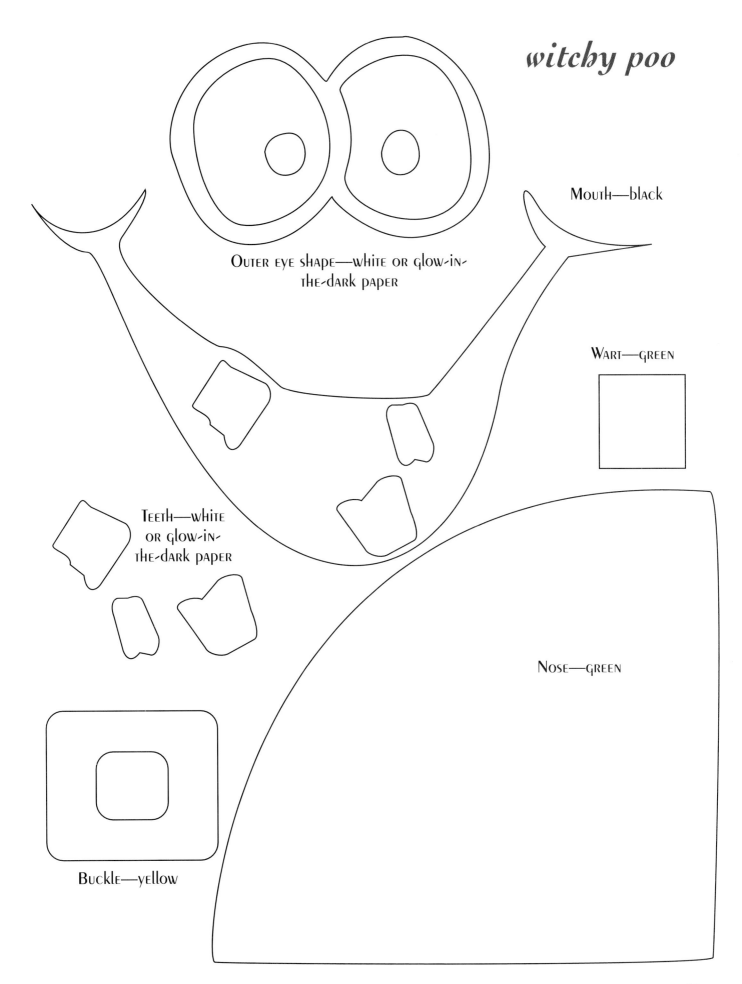

witchy poo

Mouth—black

Outer eye shape—white or glow-in-the-dark paper

Wart—green

Teeth—white or glow-in-the-dark paper

Nose—green

Buckle—yellow

mr. jack with cat

leaf

*young tom
turkey*

Buckle—bright yellow

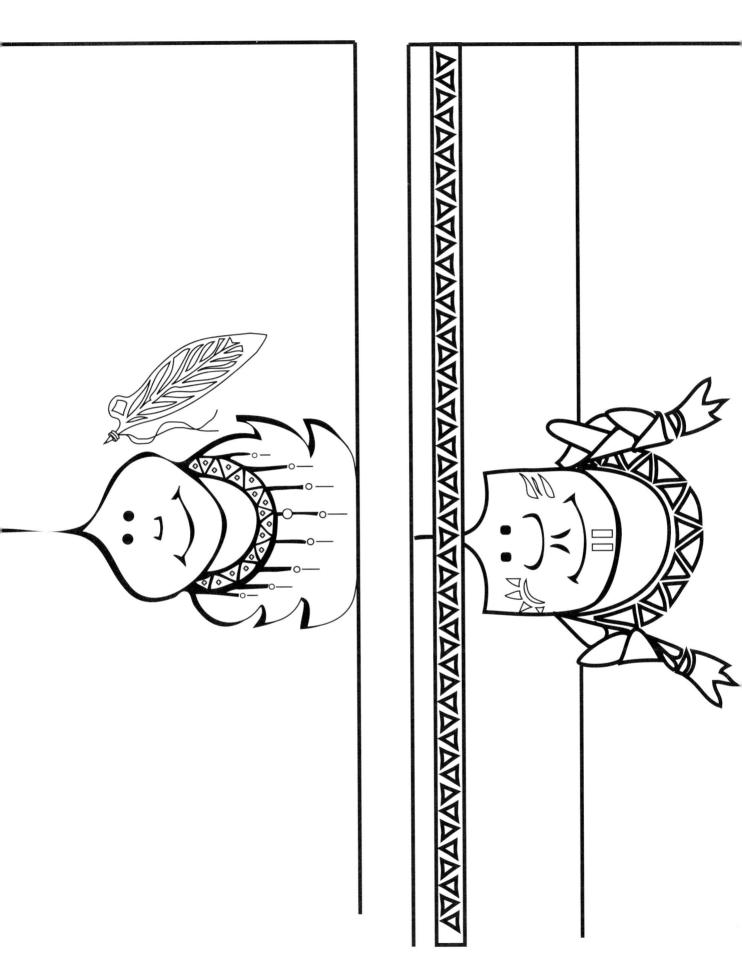

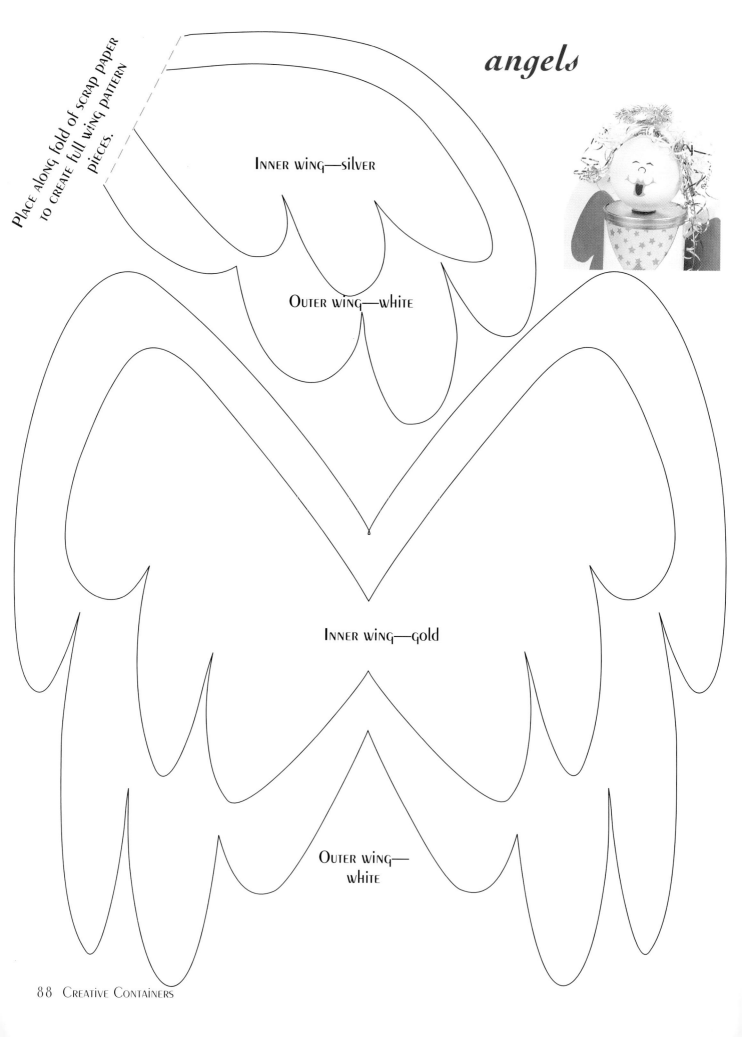

angels

Angel gowns

Cut along this line for silver angel
short gown.

Trace full length for long gown.

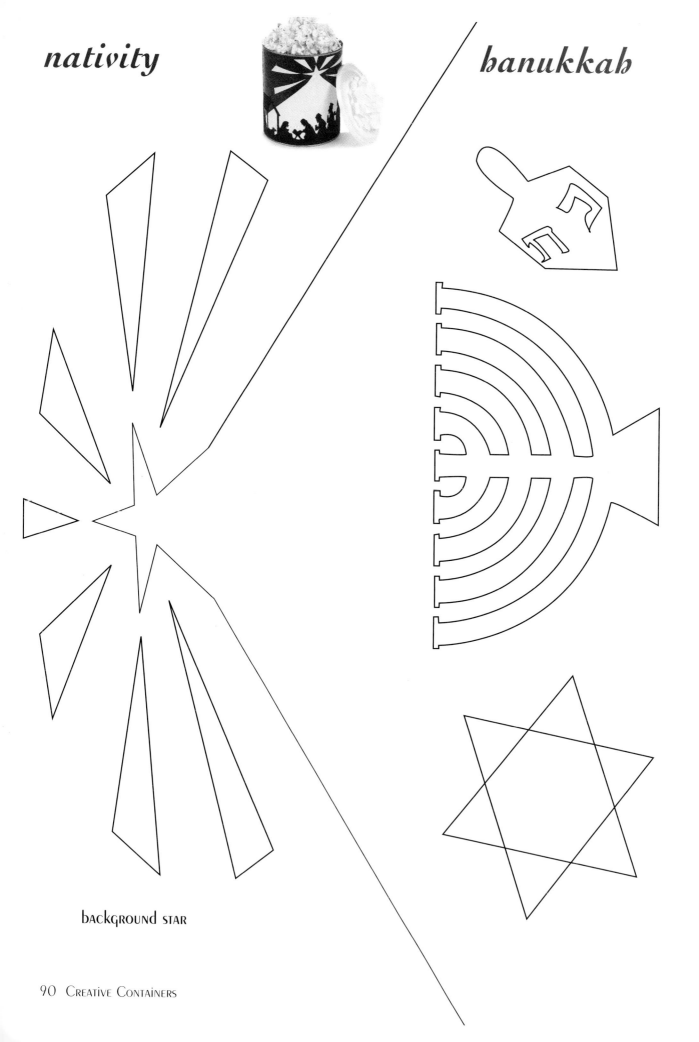

nativity

hanukkah

background star

kwanzaa

santa

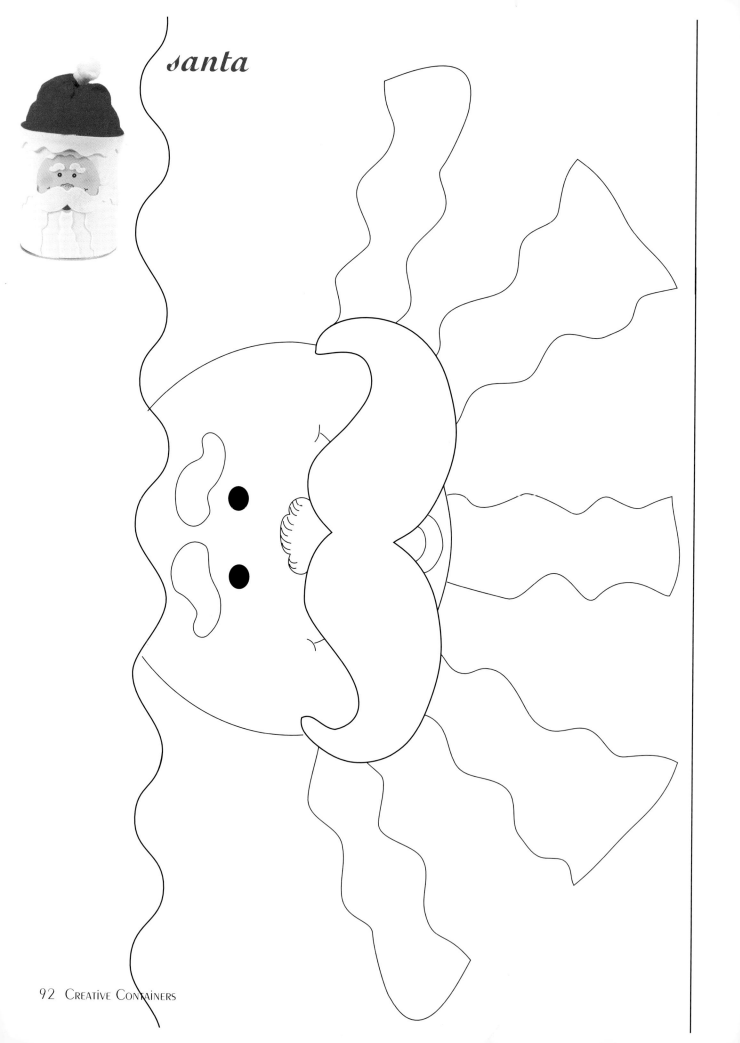

rodney reindeer

key to my heart angel bear

wings

mr. snowman

perry
penguin

foot